Recycled Pups

From rescued dog to therapy pet:

a road map to success

Lee Gaffney

Malay Ghose-Hajra, Ph.D.

recycledpups.com

Sections on pages 78-79 are excerpted with permission from Ann R. Howie, *The Handler Factor: Evaluating Handlers for Animal-Assisted Interactions Programs* (Olympia, WA, 2008). © 2015 by Ann R. Howie.

Our special thanks to
Kris Butler (dogprograms.com),
Suzanne Clothier (suzanneclothier.com) and
Ann R. Howie (humananimalsolutions.com)
for their inspiration
and to the
American Kennel Club (akc.org)
For recognizing the value of rescue and therapy dogs.

www.recycledpups.com
recycledpupsnola@gmail.com

Cover Photo: Lilou, rescued therapy pet
Photographer: Stacey Warnke
staceywarnkephotography.com

Table of Contents

Our thoughts on writing this book

The joy of adopting a dog can hardly be expressed in words. Dogs bring bliss, happiness, and an abundance of laughter into our lives. The recycled pup's *second life* is dedicated to showering us with love and affection. Many of us are privileged to share our rescued dog's love with others through animal assisted activity work. The people we meet and the residents we visit at nursing homes, retirement facilities and hospitals appreciate the non-judgmental attitude of their four-legged guests.

A majority of the dogs rescued from a shelter, rescue group or the street come with little or no background information or behavioral history. Yet, they may exhibit all the characteristics necessary to become an animal assisted activity or therapy pet. Although obedience and behavioral training is a valuable part of developing a dog's potential for therapy work, it is our belief that a true therapy pet is born and not trained.

Without proper guidance and direction, entering and participating in the world of animal assisted activity with a rescued dog can be a very daunting task. Questions commonly raised by a novice venturing into this field are *"Is my dog good enough?", "Do I have the right skills?", "Do we have the right temperament"*, or *"Do my dog and I make a good team?"* If a person owns a rescued dog, or is interested in adopting a dog suitable for animal assisted activity work, a fundamental understanding of the desirable characteristics for pet and handler, rules and regulations of the certifying organization, liability issues, the evaluation process, the mentoring period, and components of the actual visit can alleviate many headaches and heartaches down the road.

Although, neither of us are certified veterinarians or animal behavior specialists, we have been very fortunate to rescue and adopt a number of pure-bred and mixed-breed dogs who have been great ambassadors for animal assisted activity work. Working closely with local animal shelters, rescue groups and animal assisted activity organizations in New Orleans, both of us have been evaluating handlers with dogs for therapy work and mentoring new volunteers for more than 25 years. Throughout these years, we have seen both inspiring and struggling sides of humans and pets as they mature to become great animal assisted activity teams bringing joy and happiness to everyone they meet.

By writing this book, we intend to share our experiences with you as we continuously strive to become better animal assisted activity teams with our own rescued dogs. We hope our life experiences will help make you and your pooch a well prepared and confident team as you enter the wonderful world of animal assisted activity work.

Lee Gaffney
Malay Ghose-Hajra, Ph. D.

Dedicated to

the Visiting Pet Program
of New Orleans
(www.visitingpetprogram.org)

Our special thanks to the devoted teams who,
since 1987,
have lived up to their motto of

"Bring Love and Leave Smiles"
to nursing homes and hospitals
in the greater New Orleans area.
Many of the members of the VPP
generously shared their time,
talents and photos
to make this book a reality.

Since 1987

Lagniappe

la·gniappe - *noun* \'lan-,yap, lan-'\ (*LAN-yap*)

Definition: a small gift given to a customer by a merchant at the time of purchase - Merriam Webster Dictionary on line.

Lagniappe is a word that carries the flavor of southern hospitality and is frequently used in the Louisiana dialect. The lagniappe in "Recycled Pups" includes heart-warming stories of rescued therapy dogs who have touched the lives of many individuals. The positive effects of the dog's unconditional love on human health have been well documented through research and observations. The "lagniappe" stories included in this book originate from personal experiences of rescued therapy dog handlers whom we have known for several years. These dedicated human volunteers and their loyal canine partners take pride in giving that "extra" gift of love and affection, which is so vital to our well-being and emotional enrichment. It is our hope that these inspirational stories will motivate you to share your dog's love with others.

As members of a pet therapy team, it is both our responsibility and honor to share the gift of unconditional love from our recycled pup. As you and your rescued pooch continue to spread love, heal others and enrich the quality of their lives, share your personal stories with everyone - young and mature. Be proud of your accomplishments and always thank your canine partner for his selfless work. Let your personal story be an inspirational lagniappe for a new pet therapy team.

How we got into animal assisted activity work

"It's been said that animals open doors so that healing can begin. Let us humans always listen so that we hear opportunities knocking on those doors, and creatively work with dogs to walk through— then discover the endless possibilities inside."

Kris Butler,
from her speech as she accepted Delta Society's 1995 Therapy Dog of the Year Award with Partner

Molly and Lee

Her name was Molly. She wasn't much to look at but she grabbed my heart the minute I saw her at the local animal

Molly
Photo by Mitchel Osborn Photography

shelter. Her adoption was accidental. . . I had taken my mom on the shelter tour to find a dog for her. Mom came home empty handed; I got Molly, a 7-month old, white, fuzzy-haired, scared puppy.

We soon learned Molly was afraid of men. My patient, sweet, gentle husband and active teenage son helped her get over her fears. Her personality and confidence blossomed. She grew to love all people and sought out their attention. She enjoyed the company of other dogs and soon became a big sister to our next rescue, Magoo.

In the late 1980's, the word "pet therapy" (as it was called then) began to creep into the vernacular of the animal scene in New Orleans. In 1991, I learned that the Louisiana SPCA had started a small program. Molly and I were anxious to become a part of the program.

We were evaluated for our appropriateness as a pet therapy team. Molly passed with flying colors. After a few test visits, we officially became members of the group. My Molly was a natural, the consummate professional. She would enter the visiting room of a facility, survey those she was to visit, decide on her own who needed her most, and then head straight to that person. My only role was to drive her there and hold the leash. She did all the work and she taught me something new on every visit.

One sunny, hot Saturday morning, we visited the children's wing at a large hospital. As always, we started going room to room. As we started to enter one particular room, a nurse stopped us and said, "No reason to go in there. The little girl is in a coma." Undaunted, Molly nosed her way into the room where we met the mother who told us that her daughter had been hit by a car while riding her new bike on her birthday 10 days earlier. Mom explained that her daughter loved dogs and asked that I put Molly in the bed just to be with her daughter. I explained to Molly that the little girl was sleeping really, really hard. Molly snuggled close and immediately started to gently kiss the sleeping child on the face in an effort to wake her up, just like she woke me up every morning.

Suddenly, the child's closed eyes started to twitch like she was trying to open them. The mother and the nurses in the room stated screaming with excitement. It was the first indication that the child was able to feel and understand. With that inspiration, I moved Molly around the bed and instructed the child to pet the dog. To everyone's amazement, the child picked up her arm and tried to reach for Molly. Molly was as still as she could be. She knew it was an important time and that she had important work to do. The previously unresponsive child reached out for Molly every time we moved her. Everyone now knew that the still comatose child was able to hear and follow directions; it was the ray of hope the family and medical staff desperately needed.

Needless to say, after that experience I was hooked on pet therapy. I have spent the next 20+ years visiting a variety of facilities, providing animal assisted activity to people of every background and age group. I recently had my twelfth dog evaluated as a therapy pet. That little group of seven volunteers that originally welcomed me and Molly has grown to more than 100. In 2000, it became a full-fledged non-profit organization, the Visiting Pet Program.

When I think back on how much I have grown in my people skills as well my dog skills, I have to contribute a large portion of my success to that white, wiry, little dog named Molly. Her compassion, instinct and unconditional love opened my eyes, and the eyes of many others, to the wonders of animal assisted activity work.

Mita and Malay

I named her Mita. The word "Mita" means female companion in an Asian-Indian language. In April 2006, Iberia Humane Society of Louisiana found Mita as a stray. She was taken from the shelter by volunteers from Gulf South Golden Retriever Rescue (GSGRR). During a visit to her foster home, I was immediately smitten by the charm and beauty of this petite blonde. I also quickly recognized Mita's potential to be a wonderful therapy dog. After adopting her from GSGRR, I enrolled her in

Mita

obedience training classes where she responded very well to the training and received the Canine Good Citizen certification from the AKC.

In early 2007, Mita and I passed the Volunteer Pet-handler evaluation and became a Certified Animal Assisted Activity team with the Visiting Pet Program (VPP) in New Orleans, Louisiana. Since then, Mita has visited several nursing homes and assisted living facilities in the New Orleans area with me. Mita loves her visits and brings a smile to everyone who crosses her path. She loves to be petted and enjoys giving doggy kisses. Mita was also selected by the Board of VPP to visit the Children's Hospital of New Orleans, a task given to the most stable dogs with wonderful temperaments. She took the challenge gracefully and, during her visits, brought a lot of joy and happiness to the lives of the ailing children. In March of 2008, in recognition of her exemplary dedication to therapy work, Mita earned the "Outstanding Volunteer" award presented by the Board of VPP at their annual meeting.

Mita's therapy work is not limited to humans. At home, she welcomes frightened, mistreated, dirty, and distressed Golden Retrievers with wagging tails. With her help, these foster dogs soon become loving and trusting companions who are then adopted to families all over the United States. Since coming to my house, Mita has helped rehabilitate several hundred rescued Golden Retrievers. She travels with me to pick up foster Goldens from animal shelters, or meet people who surrender their Goldens to Gulf South Golden Retriever Rescue. Every time I take a foster golden to the airport for transport, Mita is there to provide comfort to the dog before the long flight.

Mita has participated in a number of canine events throughout Louisiana and Mississippi; being the silent, but always engaging, ambassador of Golden Retriever rescue and animal assisted activity work. Young kids, adults, elderly men and women are all encouraged by her loving and comforting nature to rescue a similar canine companion. Mita also volunteers at Visiting Pet Program's Pet-handler Orientation workshops to give hands-on demonstrations about the work of a therapy dog. At home, she continues to comfort me and her canine brother, Tej, on a regular basis.

I am fortunate to have Mita in my life. She has been a truly amazing companion to me and a loving friend to everyone she meets.

Chapter 1
What is Animal Assisted Activity?

"Therapy Dogs are born not made, and training, love and dedication bring them to their full potential."

Therese Weiner, Patch O' Pits Therapy Dogs©

ANIMAL ASSISTED ACTIVITY (AAA)
VS.
ANIMAL ASSISTED THERAPY (AAT)

Human and canine volunteers involved in therapy activities come in all shapes, sizes, colors, backgrounds, and personalities. Volunteers, with assistance from their canine partners, strive to provide companionship and comfort to the people they visit.

By definition, there are two types of therapy dogs: those who work in **Animal Assisted Activity (AAA)** programs and those who work in **Animal Assisted Therapy** (AAT) programs.

As defined on the **Pet Partners** web site (http://petpartners.org/), the formal definition of Animal Assisted Activities *(AAA)* *also called Animal Assisted Intervention (AAI)* is: "AAA provides opportunities for motivational, educational, recreational, and/or therapeutic benefits to enhance quality of life. AAA are delivered in a variety of environments by specially trained professionals, paraprofessionals and/or volunteers, in association with animals that meet specific criteria." (from Standards of Practice for Animal Assisted Activities and Therapy)

What does this really mean? Animal assisted activities are basically the "meet and greet" activities that involve pets visiting people. The same activity can be repeated with many people.

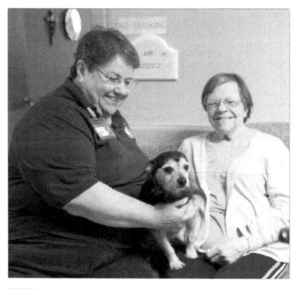

Pam Bellone and Rusty meet a new friend.

As defined on the **Pet Partners** web site *Animal Assisted Therapy (AAT)* "is a goal-directed intervention in which an animal that meets specific criteria is an integral part of the treatment process. AAT is directed and/or delivered by a health/human service professional with specialized expertise, and within the scope of practice of his/her profession. Unlike AAA, animal assisted therapy (AAT) is tailored to a particular person or medical condition.

According to Standards of Practice for Animal Assisted Activities and Therapy, "AAT is designed to promote improvement in human physical, social, emotional, and/or cognitive functioning. AAT is provided in a variety of settings and may be group or individual in nature. This process is documented and evaluated."

Dogs who work in AAT usually have some advanced obedience training and know specific skills used as part of a human's treatment process.

The goal behind writing this book is to help you turn your rescued dog into a pet who can work in a medical arena as an animal assisted activities (AAA) dog. With additional training, your dog might become one who can work in an animal assisted therapy program. The term pet therapist is interchangeable and refers to animals, in this case dogs, who work in both animal assisted activities and animal assisted therapy programs. For our purposes, we'll refer to all our pet therapists as male and we'll refer to those we visit in both hospitals and nursing homes as residents or patients.

It should be noted that therapy dogs are not service dogs and hence, by law are not afforded the same privileges. The Americans with Disabilities Act defines service dogs as *"dogs that are individually trained to do work or perform tasks for people with disabilities. Examples of such work or tasks include guiding people who are blind, alerting people who are deaf, pulling a wheelchair, alerting and protecting a person who is having a seizure, reminding a person with mental illness to take prescribed medications, calming a person with Post Traumatic Stress Disorder (PTSD) during an anxiety attack, or performing other duties. Service animals are working animals, not pets. The work or task a dog has been trained to provide must be directly related to the person's disability. Dogs whose sole function is to provide comfort or emotional support do not qualify as service animals under the ADA."*

This book focuses on rescuing and training a dog who can accompany you to nursing homes, retirement facilities, and hospitals to provide comfort and caring to the residents. As you work with your dog in these animal assisted activities, the skills learned can be utilized in other environments such as assisting a child in improving his reading skills or helping a patient heal from trauma at a rehabilitation facility.

THE BEGINNING OF IT ALL

"A pet is an island of sanity in what appears to be an insane world. Friendship retains its traditional values and securities in one's relationship with one's pet. Whether a dog, cat, bird, fish, turtle, or what have you, one can rely upon the fact that one's pet will always remain a faithful, intimate, non-competitive friend -- regardless of the good or ill fortune life brings us."
- Dr. Boris Levinson

Finding a definitive date for the beginning of the Animal Assisted Therapy (AAT) or Animal Assisted Activity (AAA) movement is quite difficult. Some articles date it back as far as 1792 at the Quaker Society of Friends York Retreat in England. It was nursing the dog "Cap" back to health in 1837 that gave Florence Nightingale the dream of going into a career in nursing. In 1860, the Bethlem Hospital in England added animals to the ward, greatly improving patients' morale. Jofi, Sigmund Freud's Chow Chow, was often present during his pioneering sessions of psychoanalysis. The US military promoted the use of dogs as a therapeutic intervention with psychiatric patients in

Jofi, with Sigmund Freud in 1937. Source: Associated Press

11

1919 at St Elizabeth's Hospital in Washington, DC.

Dr. Boris Levinson, a psychologist, was recognized in the early 1960s as the first professionally-trained clinician to formally introduce and document the way companion animals could accelerate the development of a rapport between therapist and patient. His dog, Jingle, would help him in increasing a patient's motivation and success. He is credited with being the father of the modern animal assisted therapy movement and with coining the phrase "pet therapy". *Pet-oriented Child Psychotherapy*, published in 1969, has universal appeal, from human service practitioners, health and mental health practitioners to educators in social work, psychology, nursing, and veterinary medicine. Dr. Levinson once commented, "Pets are of particular help to those groups of people which our society has forced into marginal positions such as children without families, the aged, the mentally retarded, the emotionally disturbed, the physically disabled and the inmates of correctional institutions. All of these people can suffer from isolation, a scarcity of rewarding activities and a sense of rejection. A pet can literally mean the difference between life and death."

BENEFITS OF ANIMAL ASSISTED ACTIVITIES

"The purpose of life is not to be happy. It is to be useful, to be honorable, to be compassionate, to have it make some difference that you have lived and lived well."
— *Ralph Waldo Emerson*

A smile seems like such a little thing, a natural thing, a thing that comes so easily to many of us. However, to someone in pain or someone in emotional isolation, a smile can be quite fleeting. A properly-trained dog, when handled professionally, can offer unconditional

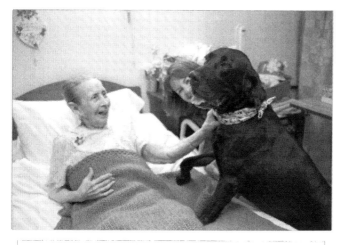

Nancy Tatarski and Moss visit bedside

companionship and non-judgmental support to someone who is experiencing physical or emotional agony. A dog can literally bring joy to a person in pain and leave a smile on their face. And, sometimes, that is the greatest gift of all.

If you have felt a connection with your dog and experienced their unconditional love and acceptance, you know the value of a dog's companionship. The benefits of AAA in reducing human stress and positively affecting our health has been well-documented. These unique canine qualities can make your rescued dog an ideal therapeutic visitor to medical facilities.

The hard science has proven again and again that stroking or petting a dog lowers the blood pressure of the human as well as the dog. *Benefits of Animal Assisted Therapy* by the Duke Cancer Institute states, "Animal assisted activities/therapy (AAA/AAT) is a highly effective form of psychotherapy intervention that has not only been shown to aid stress and depression, but provide a sense of companionship that can combat feelings of isolation. It is a cheap yet effective way to maximize health outcomes for our hospital patients. It is important to note the Centers for Disease Control and Prevention has never received a report of infection from animal assisted therapy."

Working with a therapy animal has also resulted in a reduction in depression for elderly with dementia. In *The Truth About Animal Assisted Therapy* by Brandi-Ann Uyemura, Dr. Cynthia Chandler, a counseling professor at the University of North Texas, notes that the research speaks for itself. "There is actually a psycho-physiological, emotional and physical (component) to interacting with a therapy animal." And the key that links all of these positive benefits comes down to oxytocin. In addition to lowering blood pressure and heart rate, it is a powerful healing mechanism. "Oxytocin is one of the best, most powerful, wonderful, healthy social hormones we have and it's the one that's the most grossly affected in a positive way through human-animal interaction." She says animal assisted therapy is here to stay simply because the oxytocin effect is undeniable. Therapy animals also provide a purely non-judgmental space for individuals to work out their problems. Chandler says, "Animals do not prejudge you. Sometimes it's petting an animal itself or their ability to teach us in the present moment that we find too difficult to learn on our own. But it's also the sheer presence of an animal, their acceptance

There have been many Saturday mornings when I didn't want to get out of my warm, cozy bed and make that scheduled visit. But, being true to my responsibilities, and knowing that one day I might be in a facility without my dog, I pull my achy self out of bed and head out for the visit. Once at the facility, I forget my own aches and pains. My focus turns to my dog and those we are visiting. The simple act of sharing my dog with others helps me to refocus, regroup, and reevaluate what is important.

Lee

15

and admirable ability to express themselves without holding anything back that makes Animal Assisted Therapy so powerful".

ACTION/REACTION/INTERACTION

On a typical visit, after a quick knock on the door and a request to enter, the pet therapy team will enter a patient's room. That is the action. Then there is the reaction – "oh, what a beautiful dog! What's his name? How old is he?" Which brings us to the interaction – "his name is Andy. He is three years old. It's obvious you love dogs. Do you have a dog?" The conversation will flow and continue from there. It may only last a minute or two or continue for 30 minutes. However, during that time, the person has forgotten about their pain or loneliness. The patient is focused on the joy the dog has just brought into his life. Dogs act as the catalyst to conversation; they can jump-start a relationship.

A dog also serves as the liaison to socialize at a health care facility. That cold nose will sniff out a patient in need and ultimately bring together staff, family members and visitors. The "therapy" is not limited to the residents and patients. Family members visiting their loved ones at the facility can need stress relief, too. Staff members, normally focused on the day-to-day tasks of managing a facility and caring for others, take great solace in a quick break to pet a visiting dog.

An article in the March 6, 2015 Essex News Daily talks about the benefits of animal assisted therapy/activities for the residents of the county owned psychiatric hospital,

Essex County Hospital Center, in Essex, New Jersey. *"This is a big responsibility for our volunteers to bring their pets here every week and we really appreciate it. It means a great deal to our patients,"* said Essex County Hospital Center Medical Director Robert G. Stern. *"We have a group of patients here who don't interact with others, are scared of other people or don't have a desire to socialize. It's difficult to reach these patients and engage them in any activities. We were looking for new ways to reach these non-verbal patients and have found it in our Animal Assisted Therapy."*

Dr. Dona Bellucci, a principal psychologist who spearheaded the creation of the program with the chief of therapeutic services, Michele Collins, said studies have shown that having a dog in the room relaxes patients, lowers their blood pressure and increases their immune system. *"There is something about the human and dog bond that reaches our patients. It's a meaningful, legitimate intervention from which our patients benefit,"* Bellucci said.

In the *Mayo Clinic Consumer Health* article *Pet Therapy: Man's Best Friend as Healer,* the question is asked *"Does pet therapy have risks? The biggest concern, particularly in hospitals, is safety and sanitation. Most hospitals and other facilities that use pet therapy have stringent rules to ensure that the animals are clean, vaccinated, well trained and screened for appropriate behavior. It's also important to note the Centers for Disease Control and Prevention has never received a report of infection from animal assisted therapy."*

When researching the benefits of animal assisted activity, the focus of the research is usually on the hospital patient or nursing home resident. Personal experience tells us that there are also many benefits for the therapy team. We already mentioned that science has proven that the dog's blood pressure is lowered when being stroked. The constant interaction with new people can be a confidence builder for an already outgoing dog. From personal experience, we are sure the dogs know they are working. They know this is their job. They have learned how to do it, and they thoroughly enjoy providing their own form of therapy.

For the human end of the leash, we can't help but think that our blood pressure is also lowered. Visiting with your dog is a wonderful way to meet new people, both residents and volunteers. It is also a unique way to help others. You will take great pride in seeing your dog bring such joy to others. It's also fun to be recognized by residents and staff members of a facility you visit on a regular basis.

LAGNIAPPE

A letter of thanks and appreciation

sent to the Visiting Pet Program in New Orleans, LA

I just wanted to write a letter praising your volunteers and the wonderful work they do. I have seen two pups come visit (though I'm sure there have been more) our unit- Mozart was the first and most recently I met Miss Betty Boop.

Miss Betty Boop

Though on both days my patients were being kept medically sedated and thus were not awake to have a visit, I was able to come meet the pups and wanted to let you all know how much joy having a quick meeting with your volunteers has brought me. Please never stop doing what you all do! In the midst of a 12-hour shift full of machines and bells and rushing around, seeing such sweet and gentle puppy faces provided a welcomed and much-needed break. It made me relaxed and happy and when Betty Boop put on her glasses!?! Forget it! I'm in love!

Bottom line: your services bring joy and smiles to patients AND nurses alike! Thank you! We appreciate all that your volunteers do.

Jamie Alexandra McKenna, BSN, RN

Cardiac/Medical ICU Nurse, New Orleans

Chapter 2
Rescue Dog to Therapy Pet

"Saving one dog will not change the world,
but surely for that one dog, the world will change forever."
— *Karen Davison*

A rescued dog is one that has been saved after being found as a stray, a dog that has been saved from an abusive or neglectful home, or a dog that is simply no longer wanted or can no longer be cared for by its owner and is taken in by a rescue organization. The age, gender and breed of these dogs are as varied as their story of rescue.

Awaiting adoption at the Jefferson Parish Animal Shelter

According to the American Society for the Prevention of Cruelty to Animals (ASPCA), each year approximately 3.9 million dogs enter shelters around the country. Annually, approximately 1.2 million dogs are euthanized simply because supply is greater than demand. Shelters do not have space or financial resources to support them indefinitely. Regardless of the dog's story or how you define rescue, by adopting your new dog from a rescuing organization, you are giving that dog a second chance in life. You are "recycling" that pup. (see Fact Sheet on pet overpopulation on page 163)

Cisco– ready for adoption

These "recycled" dogs can possess all the desirable qualities to become a champion therapy pet. Based on our personal experience, we can attest that some of the best therapy pets we have evaluated or encountered were rescued from an animal shelter, rescue groups, or rescued directly from the streets by their handlers. If evaluated and selected with care, these rescued dogs can turn into great ambassadors for animal assisted therapy activities. Our own therapy pets have all been rescued from different sources and each of them have taught us something new and something special about animal assisted activities.

There are a number of places to rescue a dog including local animal shelters, humane societies, or other animal welfare organizations. The quantity and quality of animal welfare organizations has increased dramatically in most communities. They are considered an excellent resource for low cost spay/neuter surgeries, vaccines, dog training, merchandise, and volunteer opportunities. These organizations are also a wonderful source of information and education. Recognizing that many animals end up in shelters or rescue groups because of solvable behavior problems, many animal welfare organizations have developed animal behavior programs or have established relationships with trainers or behaviorists. Staff members, along with the animal behavior specialists, are able to provide potential adopters with important behavioral

Pick me!

information to help assess the potential of a rescued dog to become a therapy pet. Before making a lifelong commitment to an animal, it is always advisable to ask questions about the dog's history, behavior traits, and emotional maturity. Shelter staff members are always happy to work with adopters to make sure they are matching the most suitable dogs with the best possible new owners, especially when the rescued dog will potentially be involved in therapy work.

It is estimated that upwards of 25% of the dogs entering an animal shelter are purebred, most animal shelters work closely with breed-specific rescue groups to assist in re-homing those purebred dogs who find themselves in shelters. In recent years, the number and variety of breed-specific rescue organizations has grown in large numbers. If you are looking to rescue a purebred dog, reach out to your local animal shelter or contact the American Kennel Club (akc.org) to locate breed-specific rescue groups in your locality.

Many animal shelters and dog rescue groups will also house rescued dogs in foster homes. A foster home is a place where a homeless dog receives the type of love, intensive care and attention only found in a home environment. Foster care volunteers commit to housing dogs for either a predetermined period of time or until the dog is adopted. Adoption groups often utilize foster homes to care for dogs who have special physical needs like those recovering from surgery, illness or injury. But, foster homes can also help meet the emotional and behavior needs of rescued dogs by providing a more quiet, normal environment than that of a typical shelter. Animal shelters

will use the help of foster homes for dogs showing signs of stress while housed in the shelter setting. Foster homes give the dogs the time and individual attention needed to be ready for adoption. They help the rescue groups learn more about the special traits and needs of each dog, ultimately helping them be placed in the best home possible. A foster home will acclimate the dog to a home

Louisiana Boxer Rescue foster homes provide basic manners training

environment, helping the dog learn how to behave properly around other pets, different types of people and in different "real world" situations.

A foster home can be a fabulous resource for finding a therapy pet. The foster family will be very familiar with the dog, his personality, likes and dislikes. Talking with the foster family will save you a lot of guess work when it comes to deciding if a particular dog has the potential to

25

be a therapy pet. It is advisable to build a relationship with the foster family as you are trying to learn more about the dog. Foster families, like shelter staffers, are very dedicated to their work and want the best home for the dogs in their care. Their goal is to match the right dog with the right family. Explaining the desirable characteristics of a therapy dog to the foster family will not only help them recommend the right dog for you, but also make them aware of therapy work. If possible, it is a great idea to observe the dog in his foster home and watch him interact with other dogs and people.

A question often asked by novice handlers is whether it is best to rescue a pure-bred or mixed-breed dog for therapy work. In our opinion, breed is much less important than temperament. One of the great joys of owning a mixed-breed dog is that you can get the best of all worlds! Many veterinarians believe that the mixed-breed dogs are less likely to have the health problems attributed to specific breeds. We recommend that, before adopting, you thoroughly research the breed or breeds in which you have interest to learn about any health problems common in those breeds. Your veterinarian will be an excellent resource for this information.

Another question often asked is whether to rescue a puppy or an adult dog. Our recommendation has always been to rescue an adolescent or adult dog with desirable characteristics for therapy work. It is hard to deny the charm and cuteness of any puppy – pure bred or mixed-breed. They get adopted very quickly from an animal shelter or breed-specific rescue organizations. With a puppy, you will have to start the training from scratch. It is difficult to gauge his true personality or temperament. His easy-going and loving disposition can change when he becomes an adult dog. With a mixed breed puppy, it is difficult to predict the eventual size of the adult dog. On the other hand, by properly evaluating an adult dog (pure-bred or mixed-breed), many of these uncertainties can be minimized, reducing a lot of headaches in the future. You will have a better understanding of the ultimate size, temperament, personality, and behavioral traits of your new companion. By rescuing an adult dog, you

An adoption in progress!

will also be giving him a second chance at life. He will appreciate your good deed and will be more willing to give back through therapy work.

Chances are your rescued dog is not going to come with perfect manners, ready for therapy work right out of the kennel. He probably won't be socialized to the extent

Lagniappe

Being a Foster Parent

I wanted to offer a foster home for dogs for some time but I rarely had fewer than two dogs and usually closer to six. I thought that would not be an easy home for a foster dog. When I found myself dogless at one point, I knew it was the right time to concentrate on fosters. So many dogs come from sad conditions and have to face difficult obstacles on their way to becoming secure, loving pets.

There are many scary things to face on their way to wellness. Many have never encountered televisions, glass doors and windows, stairs, tile floors, much less kindness. They've never had peace, quiet, freedom from fear, decent food, or love. Foster homes are a good transition from a dog's former, usually unhappy, life to a happy home. Helping them make that transition and seeing them blossom from a fearful, often depressed, little soul and on their way to a

Alison Cook
and her first "foster fail"

Minnie

happy, well-adjusted pup is more than heartwarming – it's addictive!

As it often happens, two of my foster dogs never left – Yes, I'm what's known as a 'foster failure'! However, we've carried on with our foster work and all three of us help the new fosters to relax and know they're in a safe and happy home. I know I'll never find a more rewarding job than that of a dog foster parent.

Alison Cook
Covington, LA

WHAT TO LOOK FOR
WHEN SELECTING YOUR RECYCLED PUP

With so many dogs of different size, age, color, and gender to choose from, it can often be confusing or overwhelming for a novice handler to decide on the right dog to rescue for therapy work. In the following section, we have tried to provide you with some guidance regarding what to look for when selecting your recycled pup for therapy work. It should be noted that, even with all this information, you should keep your mind and heart open...sometimes the dog will pick YOU!

Large or small?

Any size dog can be a therapy pet. Through the years, we have evaluated and accepted dogs for therapy work that come in all shapes and sizes. They range in size from a 5 pound Chihuahua to a 150 pound Great Dane. Small dogs (up to 25 pounds) are well-suited for the job because they can be lifted into beds and can be held in the laps of the residents. However, the continuous lifting and holding and hugging can be exhausting for a small dog (and the handler). This can limit the

Joan Rey and Sue Ling ready for a visit

time frame a small dog can actively participate in a visit. Putting a small dog in a stroller can minimize the impact on the handler and the dog.

Most large dogs (more than 50 pounds), when seated, come up to the height of the bed or wheelchair. The patients can easily reach them for a head pat or a back scratch. Medium size dogs (between 25 and 50 pounds) can be challenging to some handlers due to the bending and stooping necessary to get a medium sized dog into position for petting. The size of the dog should not be a deterrent in your finding the right rescued dog for therapy work. In the world of animal assisted activities, size does not matter! The choice is yours.

The joy of mixed breeds—no two are alike!

Photo by Christy Wood

Male or female?

For animal assisted activities, both male and female dogs do equally well. During our pet-handler evaluation sessions, we place little, if any, emphasis on the gender of the dog we are assessing. Whether to rescue a male or female dog for therapy work in entirely the handler's decision. A rescued dog from a reputable animal welfare organization or breed rescue group will be spayed (female) or neutered (male) prior to your adopting the pet. This surgery eliminates the dog's ability to reproduce. According to most veterinarians, this procedure also reduces the chance of testicular or mammary gland cancers in the dog. Spaying/neutering can also help reduce aggressive tendencies in some breeds. A spayed female will not miss visits due to a heat cycle or because she is pregnant or nursing puppies. Medical science has proven that your dog will not get fat because s/he was spayed or neutered! Because of the over population of unwanted dogs in our society, and to minimize surplus dog population, we strongly encourage rescuing a spayed or neutered dog for therapy work.

Temperament?

What does matter is the animal's overall temperament. The dog should be outgoing and confident as well as calm and gentle at the same time. A good therapy pet will want to be with all people - young and old, male or female, black and white. He will seek them out and want nothing more than to be petted and snuggled. Unlike

McKenzie with Nicole Parks
ready to work

behavioral issues which can be rectified through training, the desire to interact with people should come naturally to the dog. Just like people, every dog is different. When selecting a dog, it is advisable to consider each dog individually, not by specific breed or combination of breeds. A dog that wants to be your team member is a definite winner for therapy work.

When looking at dogs in the animal shelter, request to take each dog you are interested in out of its kennel and walk him around the facility. Watch his behavior— does he enthusiastically parade around the building? Does he solicit attention from the people in the facility? Does he enjoy the attention and remain calm while being petted? Does he look like he is just "soaking up" the love? As you move from room to room in the facility, does he enter the room confidently, eager to see what's next, or is he hesitant to enter, not knowing what is ahead of him? Confidence can be developed and improved if the

Desirable qualities of a rescued dog for therapy work

Calm

Outgoing

Patient

Energetic

Playful

Confident

Enjoys petting

Predictable

Reliable

Tolerant

.

Signs of a confident dog for therapy work

Enthusiastically embraces new situations

Seeks out attention from people

Comfortable around other dogs

Accepts petting on face, legs, tail and back

dog has had a good start. A shy or timid dog will have a long road ahead in building the confidence needed to do therapy work. Ultimately, even with lots of love and hard work on your part, a timid dog may never be comfortable doing therapy work.

While at the shelter, ask if you can bring him around other dogs to be sure he is comfortable and sociable. If the pup missed out on socialization opportunities early on in his life, it may be difficult to provide the amount of socialization necessary to help your dog adjust to working closely with other dogs. You want a dog that is happy to be around people and pets.

Robin Beaulieu, Director of the Jefferson Parish Animal Shelter, takes a pup out for a stroll.

Therapy dogs are expected to be reliable and predictable. You must have confidence in the dog to know that, when in an awkward situation, your dog will act appropriately. A dog may startle at loud, noisy medical equipment but should recover quickly without reacting (trying to bite the equipment or barking at it).

Metal food bowls are plentiful in a shelter; have someone drop a bowl and watch the dog's reaction.

A resident may inadvertently grab your dog's collar or paw; a therapy dog cannot respond negatively in that type of situation. This is when injuries can happen. Do some "clumsy petting" on the dog you are considering; pick up the paws, tug gently on the tail, inspect the teeth, pat on the head with a closed hand, give him a big, full-body hug. These are things you can easily check when evaluating a dog for therapy work.

Medical facilities are known to be chaotic at times. A therapy dog must be able to tolerate all the new sights and sounds without being reactive. Test your perspective adoptee for these things before making a decision. While at the shelter, ask if they have some equipment that might be used in place of the needed medical equipment – a pair of crutches or a cane can stand in for a walker; a wagon or cart or

---

Handling Hints:

Patience

My dog, Meghan Claire, would go with the flow no matter what the situation. I always called her my most adaptable dog as she would adjust to whatever was going on around her. Nothing seemed to bother her. During her visits, she was perky and happy to greet everyone. Once the focus on her died down a bit and I started talking to the resident, she would find a cool spot on the floor and lie down. She knew that if her human was talking, we weren't going anywhere for a while so she might as well relax and get comfortable!

That is patience!

Lee

35

anything with wheels that can roll past your pup can be used as a wheelchair. Test your new pup with the equipment and gauge his responses to these items.

Most importantly, the dog should be patient. A patient dog will greet a new person, get and give the needed snuggles, and will sit and wait patiently while the handler and resident converse with each other. This is fairly easy to test while at the shelter. Just watch the dog's reaction as you sit and talk calmly with the adoption counselor. The dog should be able to "settle" on its own by sitting or lying down quietly as you chat with the adoption counselor. For some shelter dogs, this is a lot to ask during an initial interview. The dog

Meghan Clare
at a Reading To Rover event

may have been in a kennel for weeks without ample exercise or attention. Take that into consideration when making your evaluation. Give the dog time to relax before making a quick decision.

Always enlist the help of the adoption staff at the shelter. They will know the dog better than anyone and they will have a working knowledge of what is required of a therapy dog. The staff will be thrilled to help you find just the right dog to fit your needs. Then, let your heart be your guide. This dog will be your loving companion, your best friend, for many years to come. Be sure your choice is, first and foremost, a dog you will love, cherish and care for no matter the results of your therapy dog efforts.

Mita's Miracle

On a visit to Children's Hospital, Mita and I entered a room and were greeted by a mother trying to get her son to eat. The boy had undergone major surgery. I could see the pain and agony in his face. The saddened mother confessed that she has been trying to feed her son for the past hour. With permission, I placed Mita close to the bed so the boy could reach her. The ailing boy slowly placed his hand on Mita's head and started rubbing under her ears. Mita sat there, still like a statue, and let the boy soak up all the affection. The boy gave Mita a smile. To our amazement, his mouth opened for the food. His mom burst into tears and started feeding her son. Mita and I stayed in the room with the boy until his food bowl was empty. The mother was overwhelmed with emotion and thanked Mita for the "miracle."

Malay

LAGNIAPPE

She seemed PERFECT!

You'd think that many years of volunteering with a local therapy group and working at an animal shelter would give me a leg up when it comes to selecting animals appropriate for a therapy pet program, but that's not always the case. Take Jody, the dog that I pre-tested and handpicked to be a therapy pet. After having a perfect dog and a perfect rabbit in the therapy program, I knew what to look for, right?

Jody came to the shelter as a stray, so her background was unknown, but she seemed to tolerate the noise, chaos, poking and prodding that shelter animals endure during their stay. I made a point of walking her around the shelter to meet new friends, sitting with her in the lobby and taking her to the Community Clinic waiting room, which was like Grand Central Station (with animals). She seemed perfect! After her adoption, Jody went to multiple schools to act as a demo-dog as part of the shelter's "Show & Tail" program and was by my side at numerous shelter events promoting responsible pet ownership. She seemed perfect!

Her big evaluation day for the Visiting Pet Program was coming, so I took extra care in making sure she was well-prepared. She seemed perfect! She passed her evaluation and was well on her way to becoming a therapy pet, with only one probationary visit to go. She seemed perfect... until one random day. I was holding her in the front yard and a friend placed her hand in front of Jody's nose for a quick sniff before petting. As she was moving to pet her back, Jody snapped at her. We were all shocked—wasn't she supposed to be a "therapy pet?" Aren't those animals supposed to be amazing?

Completely losing trust in her and not knowing what set her off, I immediately pulled her from the therapy pet program and never took her to another school or event again. I count myself very lucky. She "seemed" perfect!

Now that I think back about it, on evaluation day, she went underneath a bench in the waiting room and she'd never done anything like that before—maybe she was giving me a signal that I ignored, because *I* so wanted her to be a part of the program. That's just it, *I* wanted her to be a therapy pet and she didn't. I don't think we can force our pets to be someone they aren't. We can encourage them, but if it wasn't meant to be, it wasn't meant to be—we can just enjoy them as a loving family member.

Fast forward several years. Many shelters now have pre-adoption behavior testing that can generally be a pretty good indicator of what type of temperament a dog may have. My shelter, the Louisiana SPCA, uses the "SAFER™" behavior test, but there are many others that can assist with basic assessment. A few of the observations include body language, resource guarding, touch, sensitivity and eye contact (or lack of).

When my family was looking for our next dog to adopt, we first decided on breed, sex and size, then personality. This time we had the added luxury of knowing the results of her behavior test and it just confirmed what we'd already observed and was very reassuring.

Just like Jody, prior to her official Visiting Pet Program evaluation, we took Lizzie Dele to several stores to introduce her to new people, smells and situations, registered her for an obedience class and she went to multiple schools to act as a demo-dog as part of the shelter's "Show & Tail" program. She was by my side at numerous shelter events

Lizzie Dele

promoting responsible pet ownership. She seemed perfect!

Lizzie Dele passed her therapy dog evaluation with flying colors. She did really well during her probationary period, so now she is an official certified therapy pet.

She is perfect! I feel she was born to be a therapy pet and just needed a little guidance from me.

Lori Haeuser and Lizzie Dele
Metairie, LA

PREPARING YOUR NEW PET FOR THERAPY WORK

"A dog is not a thing. A thing is replaceable.
A dog is not.
A thing is disposable. A dog is not.
A thing doesn't have a heart. A dog's heart is bigger than
any 'thing' you can ever own."
— Elizabeth Parker

Once you have selected your soon-to-be therapy pet and have determined that he has met the criteria of being friendly, confident, reliable, predictable, sociable, tolerant, and patient, the real work begins!

It is the handler's hard work that will be the determining factor in the team's success or failure. It is said, and we believe it is true, that therapy dogs are born, not made. It is up to the handler to put in the hard work, do the required training, and provide the love and dedication that will bring the dog to its full potential as a therapy pet.

What's involved? <u>The first stop</u> should be a visit to your favorite veterinarian's office.

> **Things to discuss with your veterinarian**
> * *Does the dog have a medical condition that will prevent him from doing therapy work?*
> * *Is the dog allergic to any foods or chemicals?*
> * *Is the dog medically fit to perform tricks*
> * *Does the dog have heartworms or other parasites?*
> * *Is the dog's temperament suitable for therapy work?*
> * *What kind of food would you prescribe for the dog?*

41

It is beneficial to establish a close, working relationship with your veterinarian from the very beginning. Talk to the doctor about your hopes and dreams for your rescued dog as a therapy pet. The rescued dog may come to you having been given all the required vaccinations

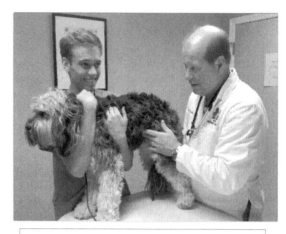

Dr. Scott Abadie gives Gabby her annual check up

and a checkup, but we recommend that you still make a special trip to your personal veterinarian to introduce the dog and discuss your plans. Your veterinarian will be an excellent resource for you throughout the dog's entire life.

Learning "down" at a basic obedience class

Next stop: Enrollment in a basic obedience training class. Learning to work as a team is of paramount importance and a basic obedience training class will give you and your dog the knowledge and practice to harness that skill.

A variety of dog training books are available to help you teach the dog basic obedience commands like sit, stay, come, etc. However, enrolling in a live class will offer you and your dog the opportunity to learn the commands in an environment full of distractions such as other dogs, people, and noise – all very common during a regular pet therapy visit. Learning in a group setting will reinforce your training, and will teach your dog to listen to you over all those other distractions. Basic commands such as sit, down, stay, come, leave it, and no jump must be part of your dog's repertoire.

Earning the AKC title of Canine Good Citizen (CGC) (discussed more in Chapter 8) is an

Components of Canine Good Citizen (CGC) evaluation

1. Accepting a friendly stranger

2. Sitting politely for petting

3. Appearance and grooming

4. Out for a walk (walking on a loose lead)

5. Walking through a crowd

6. Sit and down on command and staying in place

7. Coming when called

8. Reaction to another dog

9. Reaction to distraction

10. Supervised separation

excellent goal to set for yourself and your dog while taking the basic obedience training class. Earning a CGC title is not equivalent to having a therapy dog certification and it is not a true indicator whether a dog will make a good therapy pet. It does, however, help to better prepare your canine team for the things you may encounter while working as a pet therapy team.

Another great confidence builder for your rescued dog is an agility class (nadac.com or usdaa.com). Learning to master jumps and tunnels can be a real boost to your dog's self-esteem and confidence. Mastering the agility course also requires great teamwork. It's an excellent way to build the bond between you and your dog. It will also teach you to read his nonverbal cues, thus strengthening your relationship. The popular sport of "Barn Hunt" (www.barnhunt.com) is another great way to have fun with your dog and build on that blossoming

McKenzie flies through the tire jump at her Agility for Fun class

connection. Teaching your dog to do tricks will enhance your relationship and add some fun things to do during your animal assisted therapy visits. Chapter 9 discusses some basic trick training ideas.

Making new friends!

Socialization

Socialize, socialize, socialize! Do anything you can to expose your rescued dog to new places, people and environments. Take your dog with you wherever you can. It is a good idea to introduce your dog to people of diverse gender, age, skin color, and in different clothing. Always have soft, highly desirable treats (small bits of hot dogs or chicken) with you to reward his excellent behavior when he meets someone new or behaves well in a new environment. We've known people with creative ideas to introduce new environments to their dogs, *e.g.* taking the dog to a pet store or sitting on the steps of a local museum on a beautiful Sunday afternoon. People are coming and going, cars and noise from the crowd add ambience. Most people will stop to pet the dog. By including yummy treats from the passers-by, your dog will soon learn that good things come from new people.

Verbal praise is a fabulous reward in itself. With those good treats, always tell your dog how wonderful he is, how smart, how brave, how well behaved he is! Include lots of hugs and kisses with your praise. The more comfortable your dog is with people "gushing" all over him, the happier he will be when he is on the real job.

A beautiful day for a restaurant stop

For a little more excitement, try taking your pooch to a pet-friendly bar or restaurant. You may encounter other folks there with their pets. This activity should also include some dog-to-dog socialization. Encourage patrons to pet your dog and offer special treats to reinforce the new "good things come from strangers" lesson. In the New Orleans area, we are lucky to have many pet-friendly establishments, especially bars, filled with noise, loud music and loud people...all part of the socialization experience.

Walking your dog past a local school yard during recess time is also an excellent way to make your dog comfortable around

Ginger loves the attention from adults and children

moving activities and noise. Kids are running and screaming in excitement; the noise level can be extraordinary. Watching all the action and hearing all the noise can be a great learning experience for your rescued dog. Be prepared to sit or stand quietly with him and watch all the activity while constantly feeding yummy treats for his good behavior. Be careful not to get too close to the school yard as the kids will automatically be drawn to the dog. Their overwhelming enthusiasm to pet your pup may be a bit much for your dog at this point and could cause such chaos at the school that you may be asked to leave the area! You certainly don't want that!

Condition your dog to being touched, especially around his head. We always work on making our dogs comfortable with having their head petted and face handled. These two things happen frequently on visits. You or others can rub on the dog's nose and under his chin; rub gently around his eyes;

Handling Hints:

During a visit to an area children's hospital, my dog, Gabby, and I encountered, in just one room, eleven children from the ages of one year to 15 years! The decibel level in the room was glass–shattering loud! I froze. I didn't want to risk taking my dog into such an overwhelming situation. Gabby, on the other hand, was tugging on her leash, anxious to get to all those eager little hands ready to love on her. Trusting her, I let her lead the way. With some gentle instruction from me, the kids settled right down and individually took turns petting Gabby. I was much more comfortable and Gabby was perfectly happy!

Lee

pat excitedly on his head. Rub his ears and play with them. Add in those wonderful treats and before you know it, your dog will be coming to you for head rubs. Do the same thing for his paws and tail. These are spots that might be suddenly grabbed by a resident. Work with him to insure he does not react negatively to this "affection".

There are several simple things you can do at home to get your dog used to noise and movement of objects. Nursing homes always have TVs blaring in every room, all set to different channels! At home, you can turn up the volume on the TV or radio to simulate a similar condition. While working in the kitchen, drop a pot or pan or your dog's metal food bowl. Be ready with those yummy treats to reward your dog for not over-reacting to the sudden noise. Remember, he can react but not over-react, and should recover quickly and go back to life as usual. Be sure to reward the quick recovery, not the reaction.

Let your dog watch as you fold clothes. Shake out the big sheets or towels so that he can see them flying through the air. Dramatically open a garbage bag. Be sure it makes noise as you open in and have it flutter through the air. Have balloons in the house and get him used to the idea that the colorful thing hanging in the air actually moves. Expose your pup to different floor surfaces. He needs to learn that not the entire world is covered in carpet or tiles. Negotiating on slippery, shiny floors can be a real challenge to some dogs. Practice walking your dog on gravel, grass and concrete. Exposure to all of these things will help build your dog's skills and confidence.

Caroline Page and Buster
practicing walking next to wheels in a pet store.

Being comfortable around medical equipment provides a new set of challenges for your recycled dog. Other than beds, wheelchairs are the most common piece of medical equipment you will encounter during a typical therapy visit. If you do not have a wheelchair at home, mimic the equipment with anything you have. Walk your dog next to your wheel barrow in your yard, a child's wagon, or anything to simulate wheels and movement. Pet stores and garden supply stores will usually let you bring your dog into the store. Grab a cart and, with your dog on leash, do your shopping with your dog walking next to you. The noise and movement of the cart will help your pup adjust to the idea of things moving next to him. If you have access to a wheelchair, introduce your dog to it gently. Before anyone gets in the chair, let the dog smell it thoroughly. Offer treats if he is comfortable with the sniffing. Then sit in the chair. Let your dog absorb the fact that you are in the chair. As you sit in the chair, move it slowly away from the dog. Don't make any sudden movements. Do things gently and slowly. Analyze your dog's comfort level. If he seems to be doing just fine, increase your movement in the chair and offer treats and praise. If he's uncomfortable, stop the activity for a while and get back to it at another time, starting from square one. Just leaving the chair in the room for him to sniff and getting used to may be very beneficial to improving his comfort level. Whatever you do, don't push the issue. Let your dog gradually build up his confidence around the chair. Before you know it, he will be sitting in the chair with you.

During a visit to a nursing home, your dog will meet residents who will be resting on their bed. Most dogs are quite comfortable around beds, so getting them used to a bed is usually not an issue. If Fido usually sleeps with you, he must learn that hospital beds are off limits for jumping. As a therapy pet, he needs to learn to look up to you for direction.

Always remember you are the leader of this pet-handler visiting team. As you train, go to different people's homes and have a friend play the patient in the bed. Have your dog in control and by your side as you approach the bed. Be ready to offer a "no jump" cue if your dog even thinks about jumping on the bed. Keep eye contact with him and offer him praise and good direction. With lots of practice, he'll soon understand that only your bed is okay for jumping. More about bed etiquette is covered in Chapter 6.

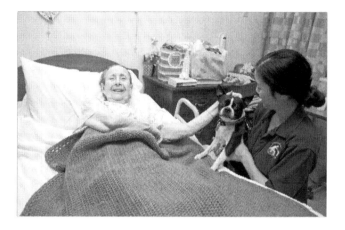

Jamie Parker and Poochie visit bedside

Walkers, canes and crutches can provide challenges for some dogs, especially those that have suffered abuse in their life prior to coming into your loving home. Using a gradual approach when introducing your dog to these items will pay dividends. If you don't have any of these at home, borrow them from a friend. If you are able to get a walker, be sure to put tennis balls on the bottom of it. Some dogs just love to go after those tennis balls and that has real potential for injury to the resident. Just as with the bed, your dog needs to learn that there are good tennis balls and "off limit" tennis balls. The "leave it" cue will come in handy here.

To introduce the cane or walker, place the item in a room and let your dog approach at his leisure. Don't force him to investigate or push him to approach the equipment. Throw some treats in the area near the equipment so that her learns there are good things around the equipment. As he investigates the new thing, offer lots of verbal praise for being brave. Gradually, as he becomes comfortable with the presence of the item, you can start moving it, gently, gradually and calmly, using it as you would a piece of medical equipment.

Offer praise and treats for his good behavior. With careful introduction, eventually your pup should be quite confident around these items. Be sure to never startle your dog with any of these items. The re-learning process can be daunting and some dogs may never quite get over that initial fear.

You probably don't have an elevator at

*Maggie, Olive and Cozette
are off for an elevator ride.*

home but you are very apt to encounter an elevator on your visits. It is a great idea to find access to an elevator and get your dog used to riding in it. The sensation of the floor falling out from under the feet can be pretty terrifying for a dog. Start out by entering and exiting the elevator several times while it is stopped. Be sure to use your happiest voice and make it a game. Serve treats. When you feel that part has been successful, try taking a short ride up one floor. Gauge your dog's demeanor. If all is going well, try another floor. Treat, applause, and praise while riding the elevator. Make the elevator ride the highlight of your dog's day!

It is a great idea to walk through a hospital or nursing home by yourself to look at the facility from your dog's point of view. Look for obstacles that might be intimidating to him; hazards that need to be avoided. Check out the floor surfaces, the types of doors you enter and exit through, types of garbage cans and where they are located, laundry carts, musical/movable art work; anything that is out of the ordinary compared to your dog's usual world at home. It will be an eye opening experience for you and a great benefit to your training and preparation as a therapy team.

The challenge is yours. The success of the training is up to you. With time, patience, and sustained effort, you can turn your rescued dog into a confident therapy pet. The poised pet-handler therapy team will then be prepared and ready for the actual visit. Both of you will be eager to spread the love and bring smiles to everybody.

Chapter 3
The Human End of the Leash

"...when comparing the handler and the animal ends of the leash, it is the handler who has the greatest potential to do harm"
from The Handler Factor by Ann Howie, LIDCSW, ACSW

The success of a therapy team is dependent on the chemistry and understanding between the handler and his pet. The handler can often play a more significant role in determining the success of the team. The best way to describe a good handler is someone who is *Respectful* – respectful of the people he is visiting; respectful of the rules of his organization and the rules of the facility being visited; and respectful of the dog and his needs. A rescued dog can reach his maximum potential as a therapy pet under the guidance and supervision of a poised and skillful handler.

RESPECTFUL OF THE PEOPLE YOU ARE VISITING
"Be kind, for everyone you meet is fighting a hard battle,"
-Ian Maclaren

Whether you and your rescued therapy pet are visiting the residents at a nursing home, patients in a medical clinic, kids at a children's hospital, or young adults at a library, being respectful of the people you are visiting is the golden rule of animal assisted activity. A sensible handler is always mindful of the physical and psychological limitations of the residents due to age, medical condition, or emotional turmoil.

Jamie Parker and Poochie visit by bending down next to the wheel chair

A nursing home or rehabilitation center can sometimes feel like an institution. It is important to remember that the facility is the resident's home and you are an invited guest. As a handler, your manners and behaviors will reflect not only upon your pet team but also on the organization you are representing.

During the visits, you will meet a lot of very interesting and remarkable people. Every resident at the facility will have his own story to share. The best way to learn about these amazing residents is to take the time and listen to them. You should be genuinely interested in others and engage confidently and naturally in conversation with them. It helps to make eye contact and use a pleasant tone of voice. Put distracting thoughts aside and smile as you approach the

When you enter a room, instead of saying this...
Hello, Mr. Smith. How are you feeling today?
Say this...
Hello, Mr. Smith. It is so good to see you today!
When you exit, instead of saying this...
Bye, Mr. Smith Hope you feel better.
Say this...
Bye, Mr. Smith. Thanks for letting us visit.

resident. Paying attention to the person's body language will help you lead the conversation and encourage the person to continue sharing his story. Nodding in approval and using verbal comments like "yes" and "uh huh" will put the resident at ease.

Another way to encourage conversation is to reflect what has been said by paraphrasing. "Sounds like you are saying........" is a great way to reflect back. Allow the resident to finish each sentence before interrupting with questions. Treat the other person in the same way you want to be treated. It is a great idea to put yourself in the other's shoes when you visit and interact with the residents.

People may have different reactions to you and your dog. The polite thing to do is to forgive their differences and accept their behavior. It is always appropriate to ask the residents if they would like to visit with your pet. Never force

Ice Breakers/ Conversation Starters

•*Hello, Ms. Jane. I am Sue. Would you like to visit with my dog? She is 3 years old. I adopted her from the shelter. Her name is Fluffy.*

•*Hello, Ms. Jane. So good to see you today. What a pretty blanket on your bed (or pretty ribbon in your hair, or nice slippers) There is always something you can compliment.*

•*Hello, Ms. Jane. Look who I brought to visit with you today! Is that picture of your dog? What was his name?*

Desirable qualities of the handler

- *Calm*

- *Friendly*

- *Confident*

- *Positive*

- *Poised*

- *Respectful*

- *Flexible*

- *Eager to serve*

- *Willing and able to meet commitment*

- *Good communication skills*

- *Good listening skills*

- *Excellent handling skills*

- *Obvious bond between dog and handler*

your pet on a resident. If someone refuses your invitation to meet your dog, politely excuse yourself and move on to the next person. Don't react or engage in a debate or ask any questions. And, don't take it personally! Just remove your dog and yourself from the situation. There will be other residents who will welcome you and your dog.

It is important that you arrive ahead of time for your visits. Keep your attire appropriate and accessories simple and low key. The focus of the visits should be about caring for other people and not making a fashion statement. This is not the time for high heels, low cut tops, short shorts, or muscle shirts. There will be lots of walking, bending over, carrying, and stooping so it helps to be comfortable and relaxed! If you are part of a sponsored therapy organization, wear their uniform and identification badge. Wear them with pride – you have earned it through hard work and the rigorous evaluation process. Wearing perfume on you or your dog is not recommended during the visits, as it may cause allergic reactions to some people.

Once you become a regular visitor at a facility, the residents will look forward to your visits and will grow to depend on them for their emotional rehabilitation. In many instances, you and your pooch are their only visitors. They will cherish their time with you and your dog and will get emotionally attached to your pet. You will also find that your dog will grow to look forward to going on his visits. It is important to make a personal commitment to your required monthly visits before getting involved in pet therapy work. As the handler, you are the connection between the eager residents and your therapy pet. Don't disappoint the residents or your dog.

Visiting Etiquette

- *Do not use cell phone during visit – place cell phone in vibration mode*

- *Be knowledgeable about the facility's pet visiting protocols*

- *Check with facility regarding photography policies*

- *Strictly follow confidentiality regulations between residents and therapy team*

- *Be aware of any additional accessibility restrictions for your therapy team*

RESPECTFUL OF THE RULES OF YOUR ORGANIZATION AND THE RULES OF THE FACILITY

As invited guests, you and your dog should follow any rules and regulations of the facilities you visit. Similarly, if you belong to a therapy dog organization, it is important to also abide by their guidelines and protocols. Little gestures of respect can go a long way. For example, wear your identification badge at all times and put your cell phone on vibrate and keep it in your pocket. It is impolite to look at your cell phone for messages or emails during the visit. Your focus should be to encourage your dog to interact with as many residents as possible and make every visit a successful one.

Some facilities may have additional regulations beyond those followed by your organization. There may be areas of the facility that are strictly off limits to the dogs. In some facilities, an escort is provided for you, not just to guide you as to where to go, but also to be sure you are not going into restricted areas. A wandering volunteer with a dog can cause a lot of chaos in a health care facility!

A facility may require each volunteer to sign a contract that explicitly lays out what is expected of the volunteer and the rules of the facility. Read it carefully. Be sure you can agree to the rules and regulations before you misuse the facility's time that would be involved in training you.

Attend their volunteer orientation session with enthusiasm and adhere to their etiquettes.

The Health Insurance Portability and Accountability Act of 1996 (a/k/a HIPAA) protects the privacy of everyone's health care. As a volunteer, you may be asked to sign a confidentiality agreement. At the very least, you will be instructed that anything you see or hear in a facility is expected to be kept in the strictest confidence. Never ask a patient what is wrong with them. If the patient should share some information with you, it is not to be shared with anyone else.

Confidentiality is of the utmost importance!

A Visiting Pet Program group ready to visit at an area nursing home.

HIPAA regulations also limit your ability to take pictures in a facility. The temptation to have a lasting memory of your dog snuggling with a favorite resident can be a tough temptation to resist. Check with the facility regarding their policy on taking photos and check with the residents *before* you bring the camera out!

If you are representing a therapy pet group during the visit, respecting the organization's instructions and principles is of utmost importance. Common guidelines followed by many pet therapy organizations during the visit are:

- *Wear the organization's designated uniform and identification badge during the visit*
- *Bathe and groom your dog within 24-48 hours of the scheduled visit*
- *Arrive early at the facility. This will give adequate time for the different dogs to get comfortable with each other.*
- *Walk your dog outside the facility prior to your visit. Clean up after your dog.*
- *In case of an incident at the facility, know who to contact within the organization*
- *Be friendly and polite to fellow volunteers and people working at the facility*

You and your therapy pet act as ambassadors for your pet therapy organization every time you wear the uniform and badge. Your conduct and your pet's behavior will reflect upon the association. Being respectful of the organization's guidelines and following their protocols will not only make you an outstanding pet-handler team, but will also promote the work of your group in the community.

RESPECTFUL OF YOUR DOG AND HIS NEEDS

"It's not just how well they are trained; when it comes to therapy dogs, it's how well they are handled."

Brandon McMillan
Lucky Dog on CBS

During a visit, you and your dog should function as a team. You both want to make a good impression on the residents. Your efforts as a handler will determine the success or failure of your team, no matter how perfect your dog is for therapy work. As his handler, you need to have an innate sense of your dog's comfort levels and abilities. Being in tune with your dog will make a huge contribution to your dog's happiness and success when he visits.

Your dog should be recently bathed, odor, perfume and

Angelle, ready for her St. Patrick's Day visit

parasite-free with trimmed nails, clean ears and combed hair. Your leash and collar should be limited to those recommended by your organization. It is recommended that you always carry a waste bag with you and be prepared to clean up after your dog. Costuming the dogs is always well-received by residents but be sure your dog is just as receptive to the idea. Assess whether or not the dog is comfortable in his outfit, not over-heated, with no obstruction to his eyes or nose. Our personal dogs love to wear fancy collars for every holiday season. They seem to know they look especially dapper and love all the extra attention.

Problems arise when a handler is unaware of a dog's behavioral signs of stress. Be sure to read our section on stress to help eliminate any problems. Don't be alarmed if your pet should show some signs of

Lip licking-a common sign of stress

stress; it will happen occasionally. If you suspect your dog is becoming stressed, just excuse yourself and your pet from the visit. Always withdraw your animal from an uncomfortable situation. Throughout the visit, continue to talk to your dog. Stroke him and tell him what a good job he is doing and what a wonderful dog he is. This positive reinforcement will help him feel comfortable and will build his confidence about visiting.

After a few visits, your talented pooch will put two and two together – *"I get a bath and then I go with my human to get some special snuggles from my new friends. What a great job!"* Your dog will grow to love the work and will greatly look forward to his visits and spending special time with you.

Lagniappe

Commitment

As my dog and I walk into our regular facility, we approach one of our friends dozing in her wheelchair. We start with a cheerful "Hello, I'm here with Sadie". Our friend looks up and when she sees Sadie her face lights up with a smile. She sits up a little more straight; she is animated and starts talking to Sadie. There it is... the exact moment you realize what you do is important. You have touched this woman's heart and brought her happiness. This is also the reason you committed to being a therapy volunteer.

As you get more involved in your therapy work, you will regularly visit the same facility. You will get to know many of the people and they get to know you and your dog. Your visits will become very important to them. While some residents might not remember your name, they always remember your dog's name. In a nursing home

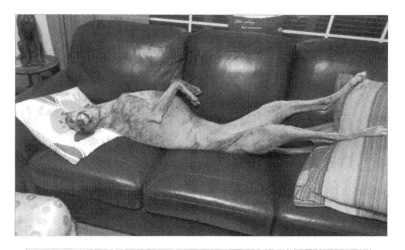

Smiling Sadie., a former racer and rescued Greyhound, relaxes after a visit

situation, unfortunately, you may be the only visitor some residents receive all month. This makes your being there for them a very important commitment.

Being a pet therapy volunteer requires an ongoing pledge of your time and energy. Therapy dogs must be bathed 24 – 48 hours prior to each visit. If you are unable to groom your dog on your own, a spa day for your dog is another time issue and financial investment. As a potential volunteer you need to think about things like this. Be realistic. Does your personal schedule and lifestyle allow you the time to participate in this volunteer activity?

An unhappy Andy gets his pre-visit bath

The group with which I volunteer requires that all volunteers make at least one visit every month. As Program Coordinator for the group, I organize more than 120 members visiting 20 facilities every month. Members are required to contact me if they must cancel and they are required to schedule a make- up visit for any missed visits.

In my experience, some volunteers take this obligation very seriously. For example, there was the volunteer taken to the hospital after falling and breaking her hip. While lying in the emergency room hospital bed, the volunteer asked her niece to call me right away to let me know what happened and that she would have to miss her visit scheduled 3 weeks later. Now that's dedication!

Then there was the volunteer couple. The female half let me know she would be out of town but assured me her boyfriend and dog would attend the visit. The morning of the visit, the boyfriend called me and left a voicemail explaining he had the flu with headache, fever, chills and could not get out of bed. That afternoon, after my visit, I decided to take my dog to a nearby park for a nice walk. Lo and behold, who do I run into jogging and using all of the workout equipment located around the park? Why, it's my fellow volunteer who called that morning to let me know he was sick! I made sure to say hello as I walked past. The look on his face was priceless when he recognized me! The girlfriend emailed the next day inquiring about a makeup visit.

As a therapy team volunteer, you make an on-going commitment. Your time, effort and dedication will reap many rewards. Studies have shown volunteers report higher levels of happiness, life-satisfaction and self-esteem. Volunteers express a sense of achievement and motivation generated from the desire to help. No one person can solve all the world's problems, but you and your therapy dog can make a little corner of the world just a bit better for the people you visit. There is no greater joy than sharing your dog with those who can no longer have their own dog. You make a difference and can be proud of your promise to help others .   *Claire Sommers*

New Orleans, LA

Chapter 4
Joining an Animal Assisted Therapy Group

"Do more than belong: participate.
Do more than care: help.
Do more than believe: practice.
Do more than be fair: be kind.
Do more than forgive: forget.
Do more than dream: work."
— William Arthur Ward

You have rescued a dog. You've done your training and built the bond. Now what? The next step is to find an organized and reputable pet therapy group. Joining an animal assisted therapy group has many advantages. The new volunteer and his pet are evaluated for therapy work and after positive outcome, are mentored by senior volunteers of the organization for a smooth transition to actual visits. There are several national and international animal assisted therapy organizations that can provide you with the framework and support to be a successful pet-handler team. Furthermore, scores of pet therapy organizations exist at a local level, whose volunteers visit hospitals, nursing homes and retirement facilities in their area. If there is no local pet therapy group present in your area, certification and volunteering through a national organization may be the best choice for you and your rescued dog.

Pet Partners
Touching Lives, Improving Health

An excellent listing of national and local groups (by state) can be found at http://www.dogplay.com/ Activities/Therapy

Dog Play

The biggest difference? In general, when you join a national organization, you will be certified to make your own arrangements and perform the visits independently. You and your therapy pet will visit on the schedule you set at the facilities with which you have established a relationship. A national organization will provide support via their webpage, email correspondences or organizational publication. For people who like working independently, this is a great way to make a difference. The positive? You work independently on your own schedule. The limitation? You do all of the logistical work and may not get adequate mentoring in the beginning.

With a local pet therapy organization, the scheduling and planning are mostly done for you. The organization contacts the facilities and sets the visit schedules. A local organization may require that you be registered with a national pet therapy organization as well as the local group. Other local groups provide their own pet-handler certification. It is common for a local organization to certify you to visit only under their umbrella. These visits are usually performed as part of their group or individually at specified, pre-arranged facilities set by the organization. For those who prefer more camaraderie, a local organization provides lots of opportunities for networking with other members in the area. It is likely that your visits will be done in groups of teams. As you visit together, your relationships will blossom and your social circle of animal-loving friends will expand. The teams provide support for each other on every visit and are there for you in case of an emergency.

The possibilities for mentorship as you visit are endless. You will learn from sharing each other's experiences and observing each other's handling skills. When a group is visiting a facility, you will notice the teams sharing room numbers of residents who really enjoyed their visit. *"Be sure to go to room 302. She really loves dogs"*. It can be quite comforting to know that another team knows you are in the facility and is looking out for your best interests.

Participation in a local group will also open up new prospects for your work as a team. As a group becomes well- known in the area

Questions to ask before joining a group

- *What is their evaluation procedure?*

- *Do they provide insurance?*

- *What are their monthly visit requirements?*

- *Are there opportunities for mentorship?*

- *Are their opportunities for participation at different venues like summer camps and reading programs?*

- *Are there opportunities for additional training?*

- *Will they permit an observation visit?*

Positive attributes of a good therapy organization

- Has written rules and regulations

- Has friendly members willing to share and educate

- Has a through orientation process

- Has a structured pet/handler evaluation process

- Will allow you to attend an observation visit

- Promotes mentoring; provides continuing education workshops

- Appreciates the contributions of its volunteers

Andy meets a Tulane University student during a final exam event

through their public relations efforts and reputation, they will receive requests for participation at a variety of venues. These may include reading-to-dog-by-kids programs in libraries, summer camps for special needs children, pet therapy to college students during final examination, and even animal assisted therapy in airports offering comfort to anxiety-ridden passengers.

In addition to the required certification, membership in a certifying organization will provide you with necessary insurance. Both local and national organizations should provide some sort of volunteer insurance to protect you and your pet when on visits. When setting up your facility visits, the first question from the facility is commonly, "Do you have insurance". You always want to be able to answer "yes". Be sure to investigate this aspect when determining which organization to join.

Before making your decision, contact a few pet therapy organizations that might interest you. Carefully review their website. Is there a pet-handler orientation? Investigate their evaluation procedure. What are their rules and requirements? Where do they visit? Are there opportunities for training, continuing education and improvement of socialization skills? Ask them if you can make an observation visit at one of their facilities. This may be a bit more difficult to do with a national organization as there may not be anyone in your specific area actively performing the visits. If it is a local group, they will usually welcome observers and will appreciate the fact that you are serious about your intentions to join.

On your observation visit, arrive early. You don't want to cause problems early on by making the group wait on you. Dress appropriately, be respectful and act as though you are already an active member of the organization. Discretely ask questions of the volunteers; never draw attention to yourself. Observe how they talk to the resident and position their dogs. You are there to watch, listen and learn to determine if this is the organization for you. Unless there is a restriction by the organization's insurance coverage, the animal assisted therapy group would be happy to bring you on an actual visit. If a group refuses your request for an observation visit, take that as an indication that this might not be the right group for you.

Based on years of experience, it is our opinion that working with an animal assisted therapy group is the best way to positively enjoy the full potential of animal assisted activity. Over the years, it has given both of the authors the opportunity to make new friends, welcome new rescued dogs to our friends' homes, share funny stories from the visits, and mourn together the loss of our beloved four-legged therapy companions. The love we feel for each other, and the support we get from our friends in the therapy group are amazing aspects of this volunteer work.

Whether you choose a national or a local animal assisted therapy group, dive in with your utmost enthusiasm and commitment to the cause of sharing the unconditional love of your rescued dog with those who will welcome a warm snuggle.

Chapter 5
The Pet-Handler Evaluation

"It's not the lead that connects,
but the connection that leads."
-Brian Kilcommon

Brian Kilcommon's statement is so true, especially on pet-handler evaluation day. That connection is vitally important when you are deciding whether or not to participate in therapy work. We have watched many evaluations where it was apparent that the human truly was devoted and wanted to be part of a therapy team. The dog, however, was actually painful to watch as he hid behind the handler, pulled his paw away when touched or turned his head away as we reached out to pet. Before you put yourself and your pet through an evaluation, have a heart-to-heart talk with yourself and be sure the timing is right for you *and* your dog.

The animal assisted therapy organization will evaluate you and your rescued dog to make sure your team will be a good fit for the organization and its core values. During the orientation or initial discussion, the organization should provide you with detailed information about the components of the pet-handler evaluation process. During the assessment, the evaluators will judge you, your dog and how the both of you interact with volunteers pretending to be patients.

The pet-handler evaluation is your first real step to becoming a certified therapy team. The first thing you should do to prepare is RELAX! Remember the rule- "it travels down the leash". If you are nervous, your dog

Evaluation Prep

- *Bathe the dog 24 hours before evaluation; trim and smooth nails; clean ears*

- *Bring all necessary paperwork and supporting documents; appropriate collar and leash;*

- *Wear comfortable, modest clothing*

- *Exercise your dog before testing to minimize some of his energy*

- *Feed your dog only a light meal at least 4 hours before test*

- *Walk your dog outside of the facility before entering the testing area*

will be nervous. That's not good for anyone! Be sure you are dressed appropriately and neatly and that your dog is freshly bathed, nails trimmed and ears cleaned. Be sure you have the leash and collar required by the testing organization.

Whatever organization you choose to join, be sure to familiarize yourself with their procedures and carefully review their evaluation process in advance of your test date. Organizations want to expand and welcome new volunteers. Their procedures and evaluation process are usually readily available on their website. If you are confused about something, contact them and get clarification prior to your test date. Don't wait! Prepare carefully!

There is bound to be some paperwork involved as part of your evaluation preparation. At the very least, there will be a volunteer application and a pet health form. There might also be a volunteer job description and a volunteer contract. Review all carefully and have them completely filled out before you get in the car to go to the evaluation. The health form will have to be completed by your veterinarian who may want to see your dog prior to completing the form. Don't wait until the last minute to ask him to complete the form for you. Think about these things in advance; be prepared and ready.

If your dog's vaccination inoculations are due to be given shortly before your evaluation, move the date up a week or so. The more time between shots and evaluation the better. If your dog was given a shot in the previous week, the area of the injection could be quite sore. When an evaluator handles your pet, he might touch the sore spot causing your wonderful pet to react negatively. It would be an unfortunate thing to have put all the effort into getting ready for your evaluation and then fail because your dog reacted to a sore spot. Don't leave it to chance. Get the shots done early.

Be aware that you, the human, are a big part of this evaluation. In *The Handler Factor, Evaluating Handlers for Animal Assisted Interactions Programs,* (Ann R. Howie 2008), Ms. Howie shares some personal correspondence from Susanne Clothier, trainer and author, who says *"What happens in the first 5-10 minutes of arriving somewhere says tons about both dog and handler."* Ms. Howie's book is recommended reading for both handler and evaluator. It provides insights into what evaluators are looking for in the handlers. We've included excerpts from her **Handler Behavioral Screening** section to help you prepare. Complete forms available for reproduction and use are published in *The Handler Factor.*

Handler Arrival:

- Arrives in plenty of time in advance of scheduled test time
- If driving, parks vehicle calmly and safely
- Unloads self, dog and equipment in a calm, orderly fashion
- Dog remains in vehicle until the handler cues dog to leave vehicle (in a controlled manner)
- Assures that dog is on leash before dog exits vehicle
- Navigates way to entrance calmly and safely with dog on leash
- Glances at dog several times or gently touches dog while approaching entrance

Handler checking in at registration desk

- Checks in in advance of scheduled test time
- Has calm, competent demeanor (not rushed, harried, or otherwise flustered)
- Places dog in position of self-control while dealing with registration process and retains control of leash
- Uses conversational tone with dog (in voice and/or hand signals)
- Glances at dog several times during interaction with person at registration desk
- Smiles at and makes eye contact with person at registration desk
- Has brought all necessary forms, equipment, etc.
- Uses pleasant conversation tone with person at registration desk

Handler greeting someone

- Uses conversational tone with dog
- Glances at dog during interaction with person

- Keeps hand lightly on dog
- Smiles at person and makes eye contact
- Uses pleasant conversational tone with person

Handler behavior between exercises
- Praises dog verbally
- Touches dog in loving/respectful manner
- Looks at dog to see how dog is doing
- Responds to dog's needs
- Observes that dog is in position or places dog in ready position before starting to walk
- Uses conversational tone with dog
- Glances at dog several times during walk
- Makes subtle changes in own pace or direction to maintain connection with dog
- Uses conversational, happy tone to redirect dog as needed (rather than yanking on leash)
- Uses gentle physical contact
- Praises dog during walk
- Praises dog at end

Handler responses to sudden, unpleasant distractions
- Recognizes that distractions can affect dog by checking for dog's reaction visually and/or verbally, physically
- Praises dog
- Uses gentle physical contact with dog as needed for reassurance or connection

The pet-handler evaluation process can be source of nervousness to some. It is always good to come prepared mentally and physically. You'll find that as the bond with your dog grows, through your training and your life together, many of these things will simply come naturally to you and you do them without even realizing. Those who have not put in the time and effort will be very apparent to the evaluators.

Most evaluations are pretty similar. A room is set up with different stations or locations that will offer a variety of challenges for you and your dog. The room may actually look like one in a nursing home. A typical evaluation might include the following stations:

1.*Clumsy petting*-while sitting on the floor, the tester will calmly and gently ask you and your dog to approach. Being on the floor makes the tester closer to eye level with the dog. If something is going to go wrong, this is probably the place. The tester will pet the dog on the head and help him get comfortable.

He will also give your dog a good "once over" check to see that the dog is clean and recently bathed, nails are trimmed and ears are clean. Then he will look at the dog's teeth, touch and lift the paws, tug gently on the tail, pat all over the body with a closed fist (to simulate petting by someone with limited

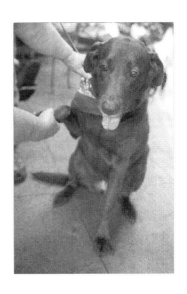

mobility and poor motor skills), and end with a big confining hug.

Your pet probably won't pass if he reacts negatively to any of this handling, is mouthy even in a playful manner, seems shy or overly uncomfortable with the handling, is not clean, has smelly ears, or untrimmed nails.

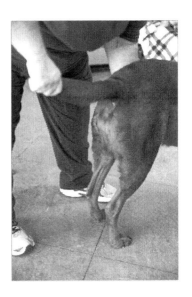

2. Walking on a loose leash – the evaluator will want to watch you and your dog walk across the room with your dog on leash, not pulling or tugging, but walking calmly by you side. Your dog does not have to be at a perfect heel position, but must be by your side, walking politely on the leash.

Your pet probably won't pass if he is tugging or pulling on the leash, is mouthing the leash as if to play tug of war or seems timid and uncomfortable walking on leash.

3. Reaction to other dogs– as you do your loose leash walking, you will encounter one or two greeter dogs. You may be asked to stop and shake hands with the handler, or just chat as you pass each other. Whatever the scenario, it is expected that your dog will not react negatively to the other dogs. Your dog should be under control so that it does not run up to the other dogs, or get overly excited and try to play with the dog. He should be at your side, able to politely walk past the other dogs.

Always pass person to person not dog to dog

Your pet probably won't pass if *he cannot pass another dog without jumping or lunging or growling/snarling/ staring at the other dog. Dogs who are over-excited around other dogs are not appropriate therapy dogs.*

4. Walking through a crowded hallway— the evaluators will be looking to see if you have appropriate control of your dog while maneuvering through people and equipment - a typical situation in a medical facility.

Your pet probably won't pass if he is not easily maneuverable through the hallway, if you have to grab his collar to direct him, if heavy leash or verbal corrections must be used to direct/control him, if he is nervous or excitable around the equipment.

5. Reaction to medical equipment-this includes a wheelchair, walker, cart , crutches, and bed. You and your dog will be asked to interact with "patients" who are using medical equipment. Remember all the things you practiced when approaching equipment. Keep your dog under good control while visiting with the patients.

Bob Klare and Maggie visit with a resident in a wheel chair

Pretend you are on a real visit and behave in the manner you would in a real life situation. Chat with the patients, introduce your dog, touch and guide him to make him feel comfortable. If you have a small dog, ask the patient if she would like to hold your dog. Place the dog on the person's lap in such a way that the dog can clearly see you. Keep your hand on the dog and the leash at all times. There will probably be people from different age groups involved in this or other portions of the test - kids, teenagers and adults - using the equipment and reaching out to pet your dog.

Your dog probably will not pass if he barks, lunges or backs away from any of the equipment, if he tries to attack the wheels of the cart or wheelchair, if he tries to play with the tennis balls on the feet of the walker, or if he is nervous or uncomfortable around any of the equipment or different people.

6. Reaction to noise—the testing room will probably be filled with noise including a television set blaring, maybe a bingo game in progress, and people calling to others across the room. As you walk through the room to each station, the tester may suddenly and loudly drop a pan or ring a bell. The tester is watching to see if your dog reacts negatively to these loud, sudden noises. The dog can react with surprise but should quickly gain his composure and settle right back into visiting.

Your pet probably will not pass if he barks, runs and hides or tries to bite the thing that made the noise.

7. Reaction to distraction—this could be any type of distraction like an umbrella opening, a walker or cane being dropped , a person running past you, or a stroller, wagon or bicycle passing by. One of the testers might even bump into you and startle you. Your dog may express interest or may be slightly startled. Remember, it's okay to react but not to overreact.

Your pet probably will not pass if he panics at the new distraction, tries to run away, shows any aggression, or barks.

8. Crowded petting-a group of three testers may approach you and your dog and start petting. There will be several hands on your dog at one time. Manage the crowd and interact with them.

Your pet will probably not pass if he is uncomfortable or becomes aggressive in this more confined situation with so many people around him.

9. *Those that use the Canine Good Citizen test as part of their evaluation will also include* **leaving your dog with a stranger and examples of obedience commands** *including sit, stay, down, come when called and leave it.* You will be able to use verbal and hand signals, and can talk and direct your dog through the process.

Your pet probably will not pass if he cannot do the basic commands or is uncomfortable, whining or barking during the supervised separation.

Important to note: a dog who urinates or defecates at any time in the testing room is usually disqualified immediately. Any dog who growls, snaps, bites, attacks, or attempts to attack a person or another dog will be eliminated immediately.

Pass or fail is the usual test result. However, some organizations offer a "not ready" category. If you receive a not ready you will be advised of the unsatisfactory issues, offered suggestions on how to correct them and invited back to another evaluation.

For all the differences in organizations and evaluations, there is a unifying factor: all are looking for safe, reliable, predictable dogs with calm, gentle temperaments who are eager to meet new people while well-controlled with gentle verbal commands from a caring and patient handler.

Chapter 6
Finally...The Actual Visit!

"Dogs, for a reason that can only be described as divine, have the ability to forgive, let go of the past, and live each day joyously. It's something the rest of us strive for."

— Jennifer Skiff,
The Divinity of Dogs:
True Stories of Miracles Inspired by Man's Best Friend

You and your rescued dog have completed the required evaluation and training and are now ready to conduct your first animal assisted activity visit to a designated nursing home. Even with all the training and hard work you have put into your efforts to get to this pivotal moment, you may be nervous and overwhelmed before entering a facility for the first time! It's okay and quite normal! However, it helps to plan for it and deal with it prior to and during your first visit. You have done the necessary prep work, passed your evaluation, and you and your dog are ready.

Our most important advice is to relax and enjoy the experience. You and your rescued dog are embarking on an exciting new adventure – be proud of your accomplishments. You should know that your dedication and participation will bring cheerfulness to someone's life today.

The first visit can be uncomfortable for both of you because there are so many new sights, sounds and smells to deal with. As you continue to visit in the future, things will start to come more naturally to you.

Your dog will soon learn that he has a new job with very specific tasks at hand. As you both continue your visits, you will become a real team in tune with each other and those you visit. Have patience and give it time. Don't expect to be perfect right off the bat. As with anything, doing it well takes time and practice. Give yourself a break!

Your choice of facility will play a role in your success. It is best to not start off in a hospital situation. Hospitals have their own set of strict rules and regulations. Adhering to all of them might add to your stress level during your first months of visiting. It's best to wait on hospital visits until you have developed your skills and are confident that you and your dog are working as a team.

Nursing homes usually offer two options – visiting in one large room with a wide variety of residents or working from room to room with each resident in their own personal setting.

Different dogs like different situations. For an older or more settled dog, the one room visit is great because there is not as much walking through the facility. Moving from person to person in a confined area is a perfect situation for some dogs. Going room to room can be a bit more stressful as there is the constant movement and continuous adjustment to a new environment. For dogs who are more active and curious, this is an ideal situation. Try both types of situations and see which one works best and feels most comfortable for you and your dog.

And don't forget the staff! Working in a health care facility can be very stressful. A brief exchange with your therapy dog can greatly lift the spirits of the doctors and nurses. You'll find that the staff will seek you out for a doggy snuggle when they know the therapy dog is in the building.

Visiting

Check

List

- *Know where you are going*

- *Know where to meet*

- *Arrive early*

- *Have poop bags*

- *Have appropriate collar and leash*

- *Be sure dog is recently bathed*

- *Wear clean , neat uniform*

- *Have ID badge ready*

- *Leave your purse in the car*

- *Have water and treats for post visit cool down*

Before you head out the door...

Remember the old Boy Scout rule of "Be Prepared"? Now is the time to be very prepared. You and your pet will both be much more relaxed if you simply take a few steps to get ready for your visit.

Make sure you know where you are going. Nothing will raise your stress level more than realizing you don't know exactly where the facility is located. Don't depend on your GPS! Do a trial run a few days before the visit. Know the route to take and approximately how much travel time is needed. Arrive early enough to have some leisure time to potty your dog and meet the other volunteers on the visit. Familiarize yourself with the entrance to the facility and know exactly where to meet your group.

Your clothes/uniform should be clean and ready to go. Be sure you wear comfortable, flat, rubber-soled shoes. Floors can be slippery. The last thing you want to do is fall! And, ladies, rule #1 is leave your purse in the car. You don't need it when in the facility. It's just something to bother you when you are visiting so leave it in the car!

It's best not to feed your dog for a few hours before your visit. The excitement of a visit can create havoc on a full stomach!

Your dog should be recently bathed (within 24-48 hrs is recommended) and combed out. Never use perfume on yourself or pets as many residents are allergic to perfume. Your dog's ears should be clean and free of odor; his nails trimmed and buffed so there are no rough surfaces.

Rough nails can be very hard on delicate skin of the elderly. If your dog is going to wear a costume, be sure to have a pre-visit fitting so that you are sure he is comfortable, can move freely and is not over- heated in the outfit.

Have the appropriate leash and collar ready to go. Use whatever equipment is recommended by your sponsoring organization and which offers you the greatest control of your dog. Having a special leash/collar designated just for visits will help your dog associate the leash/collar with fun times. His excitement for visiting will grow each time you pull out that special leash. We *never* recommend flexi-leashes as you have minimal control over your dog when he is 16 feet away! And, always bring poop bags!

Handling Hints:

Never force a dog-to-dog greeting! Some dogs are uncomfortable in close proximity to other dogs. That is why you always ask before approaching another dog for a greeting. Two dogs, like two people, just might not like each other. If that is the case, go in separate directions, on separate floors, taking separate elevators or stairwells. Do not push the issue. Keep the dogs apart and keep everyone safe!

Always keep your dog close to your side, under control, reducing the opportunity to run up to another dog. Don't allow pets to sniff each other or get involved in play.

INTRODUCTIONS: MEETING OTHER DOGS

The dog greeting before the visit and outside of the facility serves an important purpose and should not be overlooked. The group of dogs on a visit will form their own temporary pack. When a dog and handler enter the building after all the other dogs have had their initial greetings, the late dog could be considered an "interloper" and not welcome in the newly-formed pack. Chaos could erupt simply because someone was not allowed to greet properly and timely.

Renowned trainer, Suzanne Clothier, suggest a 1, 2, 3

The quick 1,2,3 greeting: count 1,2,3, tap the dog on the back and then quickly back away

greeting activity. First, ask the other volunteer if her dog would like to meet your dog. Do not continue the greeting if you do not have an okay from the handler. Both dogs should be on short leashes, close to the handlers, with both handlers paying attention to their dogs. Both dogs should be calm and settled. Ask the other handler if they are ready to greet. When you establish that everyone is ready and paying attention, move each dog towards the other and let them go nose to nose. Quickly count 1, 2, 3. Then, tap your dog on the back and **back away. DO NOT** pass each other. A quick nose sniff is all that is needed to say hello.

This brief greeting offers dogs the opportunity to give the other dog a quick sniff and satisfy their curiosity about each other. It does not give them an opportunity to get overly excited or to start sniffing other body parts.

Your dog is with you on your visit to work, not to socialize with the other dogs. How you handle the first greeting of the other pets will set the tone for your visit and all the visits to come. He'll learn that this is work, not a play date, and he will grow to love his work.

Handling Hints:

NEVER let go of your leash!
Never!
No leash, no control!

When approaching an elevator, always stand back from the elevator to allow passengers to disembark without obstruction. An unsuspecting elevator passenger can be caught by surprise by an approaching pooch!

Never allow a resident to grab, squeeze or roughly handle your pet. Gently ease the person's hand from the pet or suggest petting the dog in a different spot ..."Fluffy really likes it when you rub under her chin". Handle the situation so that neither the pet nor the person is frightened or hurt. Act on your dog's behalf for his best welfare.

Be cautiously aware of medical equipment, especially around beds.

Always ask permission before approaching a resident. It is a small gesture that shows respect for personal space.

Place a small dog on a bed or in a lap. Never let the dog jump on or off the bed or person.

For people in wheelchairs, kneel or sit next to the person so that you are not talking down or over him or her. That little courtesy helps the patient feel like an equal rather than feeling closed in with no control over the situation.

INTRODUCTIONS: MEETING THE RESIDENTS

Ask! Ask! Ask!

Always ask a resident or patient if they would like a visit with your dog. Don't just approach and assume the resident is going to love your dog as much as you do! Never force your pet on someone. Residents have varied responses to different pets. If the patient refuses your offer, politely excuse yourself and move on to the next patient. Occasionally, a patient would like to see but not touch the dog. If your pup does tricks, this is a great time to show off his many skills.

Asking "How are you today?" may not be an appropriate question for a nursing home resident or a hospital patient. It's better to start your conversation off with "Hi! This is my dog Fluffy. We have come to see you today. Have you ever had a pet?" Focus on the response. People will often want to talk about their experiences with animals. Look for something you can complement like "what a pretty blanket you have" or "what pretty nail polish". There is always something you can compliment.

Remain positive, upbeat and energetic. And LISTEN! People will want to talk, to share their stories with someone new.

When it is time to leave, close with something as simple as "Thank you for letting us visit. Fluffy and I really enjoyed meeting you." Never end the conversation with "Hope you feel better".

Speak clearly and close to the person or you may be asked to repeat yourself over and over again!

If you are aware a resident is visually impaired speak to them prior to your approach. You don't want to startle the person. Speak softly, introduce yourself and offer directions to

Handling Hints:

Children: Therapy dogs promote confidence and motivate children to interact. Be aware, however, that visiting children in a hospital setting provides its very own set of challenges. While the medical equipment is the same, the setting usually is not. A sick child is apt to have siblings visiting in the room; bored, energetic, siblings who explode when they see the dog! The room can be a source of unexpected exuberance. Before taking on the challenge of visiting children, be sure your dog is very stable and comfortable in these situations. Meeting a child or two in a nursing home when they are visiting Grandma is very different than visiting the room of an ill child and family members.

pet the dog. Ask if you can lift their hand and place it gently on the dog. Paint a picture of your pup with your words while the person is petting…"*Fluffy is 3 years old. She's a little, white, fuzzy dog with big brown eyes and a heart of gold. I adopted her from the shelter and we have been best friends ever since.*" The conversation will flow from there.

Ask which side is more comfortable for the patient to reach your pet. That question may seem a little awkward at first, but it is an appropriate one and one that the patient will appreciate. Medical equipment may hinder their use of one hand, or one side may be incapacitated for whatever reason. Asking "which side is better" eliminates the awkward moment of realizing you put your dog in the wrong place and you made the patient uncomfortable. Move your dog to the requested location to offer the best access to your pet.

Residents may ask for your assistance to move them from one place to another or to rearrange them in the bed. **DON'T DO IT!** That is not why you are there. Go to the nurse's station and explain that the patient in room xxx is asking for assistance. Always refer requests to the medical staff. If something or someone is upsetting to you, politely excuse yourself either from the room or from the building until you can regain your composure. Never draw attention to your own discomfort. Some situations can be overwhelming to even the most seasoned pro.

WORKING AROUND MEDICAL EQUIPMENT

The most common place you will encounter medical equipment like IV tubes is with people in beds. Always be conscious of the equipment location and how you will navigate around it with your dog. Because of the presence of medical equipment and a person's inability to negotiate their territory, only small, very calm dogs should ever be allowed in a bed. Residents will ask for a big dog to join them for a snuggle. However, a big dog, no matter how calm, should never be allowed in a bed. The potential for harm is far too great.

You are venturing into someone's personal space so always obtain permission before putting the pet in the bed. If you know you have a dog that is appropriate for beds, carry a small towel with you and place the towel down on the bed before placing the pup. Ask for direction as to the best location for the dog and gently place him on the bed; never allow him to jump on or off the bed.

If your dog is too big to get into the bed or on a lap, teach the command "front paws" and gently *place* your pet's front paws on the side of the bed. If a chair is available and can be placed next to the bed for easy reach by the patient, you can assist your dog getting into the chair by placing your foot behind the legs of the chair and holding it in place as your dog hops into the chair. Stand close to your dog, keeping one hand on him and one on the leash to ensure his comfort and safety while being petted.

The space between a bed and the wall can be quite narrow. You and your dog might find yourself trying to negotiate a very tight spot. This is the time that the "back up" command you learned in your obedience class will come in handy.

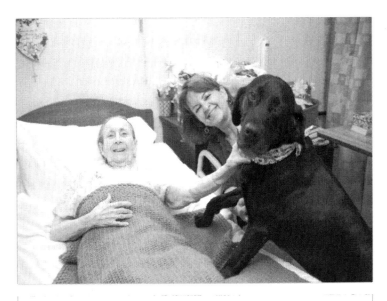

Nancy Tatarski and Moss bring smiles to a resident in a bed.

For someone in a wheelchair, your approach must be very considerate. A side approach is usually best so as to avoid bumping into the patient's feet. Be sure not to lean on the chair or move the chair without asking. Ask the patient to lock the chair so that you don't accidently move it. Don't stand over the person to talk. It is best to sit in a chair next to them or to kneel down, if possible. Angling your dog so that he is easily accessible can take some practice. You want your dog to ultimately end up between you and the chair with the dog's head near the patient's hand. When placing the dog, over step the location you are shooting for by one or two steps. With luck and practice, this will help your dog end up in the correct spot. A medium-sized dog can be taught the cue "front paws" to place his front paws on your arm or the wheel of the chair. Be sure the chair is locked in place.

Deidre Ledoux holds Mitzi comfortably
on a resident's lap. Note the towel Deidre brought just for Mitzi

Patients will frequently ask to hold your dog. Evaluate the situation before making that decision. Some people do not have appropriate laps or strength to hold even a small dog. If deemed appropriate, a small dog can be *placed* on a lap but keep your hands on the dog and the leash at all times. This gives the dog a sense of comfort and offers you the opportunity to avoid any difficult situations that might quickly arrive. Also, position the dog so that you are in his view. Your pup may quickly become uncomfortable if he can't see you. Continue to stroke and talk to your dog when he is in a patient's lap. You want the dog to remain as comfortable as possible

For people using a walker or cane, it is safe to assume there may be balance issues. To make your dog available for petting without the patient having to bend over or lean forward, always approach from the side.

Do whatever is necessary to make the dog accessible to the patient; you want the patient to be as

Maggie visiting with a resident using a walker.

comfortable as possible while visiting with your pooch.

Be ready for a workout. Making your pet accessible can mean you will be on your knees or will have your back bent for a period of time. Be conscious of other dogs on the visit especially when passing in the hallways. Always pass person to person not dog to dog. This thoughtful maneuver can help prevent dog/dog confrontations.

Kris Butler tells us in her book <u>Therapy Dogs Today</u>,(2004) *"Handlers make up fifty percent of visiting teams, but carry one hundred percent of team responsibility for the visiting process. Important handler behaviors that enhance the value of the visit include pro-active handling skills, being strong advocates for their dogs, objectivity toward their dogs, and good people skills. Pro-active handlers anticipate their dog's behaviors and direct their dogs according to what is about to happen. Re-active handlers correct and redirect their dogs after a behavior has occurred. Pro-active handlers make visiting look smooth and easy. Re-active handlers appear always to be working their dogs. Dogs are more comfortable when their handlers behave pro-actively."*

Keep all of our suggestions in mind as you encounter different people and situations. Be prepared to recognize stress signals in your pet at all times. Stress signals will vary from pet to pet, so it is very important to be in tune with your pet and know which signals apply to him. These things will happen from time to time with all pets and should not be considered a cause for alarm. When you suspect any of these stresses, withdraw the animal from the uncomfortable situation. Be sure to carefully review our section on stress in Chapter 7.

WHEN THE VISIT IS OVER

In a very short time, your pup has done a hard day's work! Visiting can be physically and mentally challenging for many dogs. Give your dog a cool down period with water and a special treat in a quiet, undisturbed place to rest and relax. After rest time, provide an opportunity for exercise and play with no mental stress. Spread your visits out. Give your dog at least 24 hours between visits. Trying to visit daily can be much too hard on your dog and may cause burn out and the end of his visiting career. You and your dog have put too much time and effort into developing your skills to let burn out happen!

Tej cools down with water, a snack and a toy after his visit

Chapter 7
Stress is a Team Sport

How to handle stress like a dog:
If you can't eat it or play with it,
then pee on it and walk away!
---- Anonymous

Stress is a normal physical response to circumstances that make us feel threatened or unbalanced in some way. Modern life is full of hassles, deadlines, frustrations, and demands. When our body senses stress, it goes into "fight-or-flight" mode. This response is the body's way of protecting us. In small doses, stress can help us perform under pressure and motivate us to do our best. However, beyond a certain point, stress stops being helpful and start causing damage to our health, mood, productivity, relationships, and our quality of life. We can protect ourselves by recognizing the signs and symptoms of stress and taking steps to reduce its harmful effects.

Like us, stress is a normal part of a dog's everyday life. Different dogs deal with stress in their own ways. However, it is important to understand that humans and dogs can get stressed differently under similar circumstances. They also react and deal with situations differently. Believe it or not, going on a one hour long visit to a nursing home with your rescued therapy dog can be a stressful event for you and your pup. Unknowingly, when we put our dog in stressful situations that they cannot escape, problems can occur.

For dog handlers, recognizing the most common signs of stress and anxiety in their dogs during a visit is of utmost importance. Learning to recognize these common signals can help a novice handler prevent serious problems down the road.

Yawning – a common sign of stress

It is also true that stress is a team sport! Emotions quickly travel down the leash from the handler to the dog. If you are excited, your dog will be excited. If you are tense, your dog will be tense. As the handler and advocate for your dog, you should know your dog well enough to pick up signs of stress. Be aware of your reactions to new situations so as not to upset your pet because dogs, too, can be seriously affected by that demon *STRESS!*

Author and trainer Kris Butler, in her book *Therapy Dogs Today,* states *"Nothing else dogs do compares to the kinds of intrinsically stressful social interaction that takes place when they visit clinical, educational or post-trauma situations. No other canine-related event, no sport nor competition requires a dog to rent her intimate zones of unfamiliar humans and remain there for several minutes of petting and hugging. Brief interactions with judges in show rings do not compare to the prolonged and repeated contact that takes place during animal—enhanced programs. Search and rescue dogs often work in chaotic environments, but not with prolonged physical contact of unfamiliar people. Service dogs work beautifully in public settings but the public is actively discouraged from touching, petting and distracting them. Humans have developed a role for visiting dogs like no other in existence. The role is new, specific and profound."*

Handling Hints:

Always Remember

YA YA BA

You are

Your animal's

Best advocate

When you see signs of stress, your dog is telling you he wants out of the environment. Your animal has told you how he is feeling; now it's your turn to advocate for him. Remove the stressor or remove the dog. You never want to put your dog in a situation that makes him uncomfortable or where the stress can escalate to fear or aggression. It can take as many as 10 positive interactions to erase one negative interaction. Avoid the negative and search out the positive.

To be an effective handler, you must be knowledgeable about signs of stress and you must take any necessary steps to reduce stress to your dog. It is your job to watch for subtle signs and leave the environment before, not after, the dog develops major signs of stress.

UNDERSTATED THINGS TO LOOK FOR...

Yawning - the first response to a mild stressor. The yawn itself is stress relieving and can help the dog release some of his built up tension.

Yawning and squinting

Panting - nursing homes and hospitals can be overly warm so a little panting is to be expected. But constant panting or panting at what seems like an inappropriate time can be a sign that your dog is experiencing stronger stress.

Lip licking – another subtle sign of response to mild stressor.

a

Lip licking

Sneezing - like yawning and panting, sneezing is a way to release pent-up

a

stress or confusion in an unfamiliar situation.

Shaking off or scratching – similar to yawning, panting, or sneezing, shaking off or scratching is a dog's body's way of physically releasing any tension that's building up inside.

Turning away/avoiding eye contact - your dog is telling you "I want out!"

Blinking and squinting - a purposeful blink or squint is a sign that a dog is mildly stressed.

MORE OBVIOUS SIGNS THERE IS A PROBLEM...

Shedding - dogs shed much more when they are stressed out as part of the body's natural defense mechanism.

Trembling - if your dog isn't cold, trembling can be a sign of extreme stress or fear.

Slow tail wag – a happy dog will have a fast tail wag; a slow tail wag is an indicator of lack of confidence and wariness.

Drooling

Whale eye – if the whites of the eyes are showing, that is a firm indicator that the dog is seriously stressed.

Drooling — stress can also cause excessive salivation

WHEN THINGS GET REALLY SERIOUS...

"Boofing" - sounds like a cross between an exhale and a bark. This can be a precursor to increasing aggressive behaviors.

Staring – also called "hard eye" or "ugly eye" is *the* sign of aggression in dogs. If you observe two dogs staring at each other, an aggressive encounter is likely to occur.

Piloerection (Raised Hair/ Hackles) and Stiffness - a warning sign to "back off"! A dog that stands still, staring intently, with its hair bristling is sure sign that the dog is not happy with its situation and wants the dog/animal/person to back away and leave him alone!

a

Tight tail tuck

Tail tucked between legs - a classic fear-signal. Feeling fearful is an extreme form of stress which can lead to a fear-biting.

Barking/Growling - there are a wide variety of barks all used as a communication tools and all indicate the need to relieve stress.

Lunging – by the time the stress gets to this point, the dog is feeling really threatened. This is the last warning sign before true damage is done via attack or bite.

Exposure to unusual noises, new equipment and/or unusual smells may prompt a worry response in your dog. Unpredictable handling or crowding by people or pets may cause a dog to start exhibiting subtle signs of anxiety. Always be alert and aware of your dog and its reaction to new things. If you miss the early stress indicators, a situation that would have been easy to deal with could expand into something much more serious. Your usual gentle, quiet dog just might turn into Godzilla!

We started this chapter with "*Emotions quickly travel down the leash from you to your dog. If you are excited, your dog will be excited. If you are tense, your dog will be tense*". Let's add to that, if you are stressed, your dog will be stressed. You need to be aware of your own stress level as well as your dog's. If you are overly stressed in your personal life, delay your visit. Take a break until things settle down for you personally. If you encounter a situation on a visit that makes you anxious, remove yourself and your dog from the environment. It's okay. No one will think badly of you. It's best to recognize the stress, remove yourself and deal with it outside. It would be much worse to push yourself or your dog into an uncomfortable situation which might ultimately end in a problem.

To reduce your dog's stress while visiting
- *Arrive at the facility 15 minutes before the scheduled visit. Avoid rushing*
- *Exercise your dog before entering the facility*
- *Keep constant physical contact with your dog (stroke his back, rub his ears)*
- *Keep encouraging your dog for his good behavior ("good dog", "good job")*
- *Keep distance between your dog and other dogs within the facility*
- *Start a conversation with the residents while introducing your dog to them*
- *Keep an eye on your dog and watch for signs of stress*
- *Politely excuse yourself and your dog from a stressful situation*
- *Remain calm!!!*

Chapter 8
Getting Recognized

"Don't worry when you are not recognized,
but strive to be worthy of recognition."
Abraham Lincoln

Most Animal Assisted Therapy teams provide their voluntary services without asking for any reward or recognition. However, the American Kennel Club (AKC, akc.org) recently introduced the Therapy Dog™ title to identify and recognize those Animal Assisted Therapy dogs that devote their time to bring joy and comfort to others' lives. The information below is directly from the akc.org web site.

THE AKC THERAPY DOG™ PROGRAM

The purpose of this program is to recognize AKC dogs and their owners who have given their time and helped people by volunteering as a therapy dog and owner team. The AKC Therapy Dog™ program awards official AKC titles to dogs who have worked to improve the lives of the people they have visited. AKC Therapy Dog titles can be earned by dogs who have been certified by AKC recognized therapy dog organizations and have performed the required number of visits. AKC does not certify therapy dogs; the certification and training is done by qualified therapy dog organizations. The certification organizations are the experts in this area and their efforts should be acknowledged and appreciated. Why did AKC start a therapy dog title? AKC has received frequent, ongoing requests from dog owners who participate in therapy work to "acknowledge the great work our dogs are doing." Many of our constituents are understandably proud of their dogs.

Earning an AKC Therapy Dog title builds on the skills taught in the AKC S.T.A.R. Puppy® and Canine Good Citizen® programs which creates a sound and friendly temperament needed by a successful therapy dog.

AKC THERAPY DOG TITLES

AKC Therapy Dog Novice (THDN) - Must have completed 10 visits.

AKC Therapy Dog (THD) - Must have completed 50 visits.

AKC Therapy Dog Advanced (THDA) - Must have completed 100 visits.

AKC Therapy Dog Excellent (THDX) - Must have completed 200 visits.

AKC Therapy Dog Distinguished (THDD) - Must have completed 400 visits.

According to the AKC website: "Therapy dogs are dogs who go with their owners to volunteer in settings such as schools, hospitals and nursing homes. From working with a child who is learning to read to visiting a senior in assisted living, therapy dogs and their owners work together as a team to improve the lives of other people. Therapy dogs are not service dogs. Service dogs are specially trained to perform specific tasks to help a person who has a disability.

An example of a service dog is a dog who guides an owner who is blind, or a dog who assists someone who has a physical disability. Service dogs stay with their person and have special access privileges in public places such as on airplanes, restaurants, etc. Therapy dogs, the dogs who will be earning the AKC Therapy Dog™ title, do not have the same special access as service dogs. It is unethical to attempt to pass off a therapy dog as a service dog for purposes such as flying on a plane or being admitted to a restaurant."

To earn an AKC Therapy Dog™ title, you and your dog must meet the following criteria:

•You and your dog are certified/registered by an AKC recognized therapy dog organization.
•Perform the required number of visits for the title for which you are applying. For your convenience in helping you track your visits, you can use the Therapy Dog Record of Visits Sheet.
•The dog must be registered or listed with AKC. All dogs are eligible to earn AKC Therapy Dog titles, including purebreds and mixed breeds. To earn an AKC Therapy Dog title, dogs must be registered or listed with AKC and have a number. This includes any one of these three options:

AKC Registration Number (*purebreds with registered parents*) This is often known as the "AKC papers" provided to a dog owner by a breeder. If you have received a registration paper from your breeder or previous owner you can register online.

PAL Number (*for purebreds who are not able to be registered*) PAL is Purebred Alternative Listing. PAL (formerly called ILP) is a program that allows unregistered dogs of registerable breeds to compete in AKC Performance and Companion Events. There are various reasons why a purebred dog might not be eligible for registration. The dog may be the product of an unregistered litter or have unregistered parents. The dog's papers may have been withheld by its breeder or lost by its owner. Sometimes, it is the dog itself that was "lost." There are many dogs enrolled in the PAL/ILP program after they have been surrendered or abandoned, then adopted by new owners from animal shelters or purebred rescue groups. The PAL/ILP program allows the dog and owner a second chance at discovering the rewards of participating in AKC events. Enrollment in the Purebred Alternative Listing/Indefinite Listing Privilege program is not to be construed as an alternative form of registration, but rather as a listing so that dogs who are ineligible for AKC registration may participate in AKC Companion and Performance Events. For more information about the PAL program, check out the AKC
web site at PAL@akc.org

Canine Partners Number (*for mixed breeds or purebreds not able to be registered*) Used by mixed breed dogs (and dogs otherwise not registered with AKC such as some purebreds from other countries). A special Canine Partners Therapy Dog Enrollment Form is available for mixed breed Therapy Dogs needing to obtain a dog number in order to receive their Therapy Dog Title. This form must be submitted together with the Therapy Dog Title Application.

Once your application has been accepted by AKC, you will receive a Certificate of Achievement to acknowledge the Therapy Dog Title you have earned as well as an AKC Therapy Dog patch to be worn proudly by your pooch!

AKC'S CANINE GOOD CITIZEN®PROGRAM

AKC offers additional titles that can serve as milestones on your training road to therapy work. The AKC Canine Good Citizen Program provides a comprehensive three level training program for you and your dog. The AKC's Canine Good Citizen Program is designed to recognize dogs who have good manners at home and in the community. This rapidly growing nationally-recognized program stresses responsible dog ownership for owners and basic training and good manners for dogs. All dogs who pass the 10 step CGC test will receive a certificate from the American Kennel Club. To find an evaluator near you, go to: http://www.akc.org/events/cgc/cgc_bystate.cfm

AKC S.T.A.R. Puppy:
The First Step in Training
You and your puppy attend a class at least 6 weeks long to earn the STAR certificate and gold medal. S.T.A.R. stands for Socialization, Training, Activity, and Responsible dog ownership. More detailed information is provided at www.akc.org/puppies/training/star/index.cfm

20 STEPS To SUCCESS: THE AKC S.T.A.R. PUPPY® TEST
OWNER BEHAVIORS:

1. Maintains puppy's health (vaccines, exams)
2. Owner receives Responsible Dog Owner's Pledge
3. Owner describes adequate daily play and exercise plan
4. Owner and puppy attend at least 6 classes by an AKC Approved CGC Evaluator
5. Owner brings bags for cleaning up after puppy
6. Owner has some form of ID for puppy —collar tag, etc.

PUPPY BEHAVIORS:

7. Free of aggression toward people in class
8. Free of aggression toward other puppies in class
9. Tolerates collar or body harness of owner's choice
10. Owner can hug or hold puppy (depending on size)
11. Puppy allows owner to take away a treat or toy

PRE-CANINE GOOD CITIZEN®TEST BEHAVIORS

12. Allows (in any position) petting by a person other than the owner
13. Grooming - Allows owner handling and brief exam (ears, feet)
14. Walks on a Leash - follows owner on lead in a straight line (15 steps)
15. Walks by other people - walks on leash past other people five feet away
16. Sits on command-owner may use a food lure
17. Down on command - owner may use a food lure
18. Comes to owner from five feet when name is called
19. Reaction to Distractions - distractions are presented 15 feet away
20. Stay on leash with another person (owner walks ten steps and returns)

Once you and your pup complete the test successfully, your puppy will receive the AKC S.T.A.R. Puppy Medal (for display or memento purposes; not suitable as a collar tag). You and your puppy will be listed in the AKC S.T.A.R. Puppy records. In addition, so that you can continue learning, you'll receive a AKC S.T.A.R. Puppy package that includes:

• A beautiful, frameable certificate designating your puppy is in the AKC S.T.A.R. Puppy records at AKC
• AKC Puppy Handbook, a valuable resource
• Discount to enroll in AKC Companion Animal Recovery Corporation, a 24-hour recovery service
• Ongoing Monthly Email Newsletter: Your AKC
This includes training tips and up-to-date information every dog owner needs to know.

Canine Good Citizen
Responsible Owners, Well-Mannered Dogs
The AKC's Canine Good Citizen program is recognized as the gold standard for dog behavior. In CGC, dogs who pass the 10-step CGC test can earn a certificate and the official AKC CGC title. More information at
www.akc.org/dogowner/training/canine_good_citizen/index.cfm

The CGC TEST consists of ten skills needed by all well-mannered dogs. All of the exercises are done on a leash.

Test 1: Accepting a friendly stranger: The dog will allow a friendly stranger to approach it and speak to the handler in a natural, everyday situation.

Test 2: Sitting politely for petting: The dog will allow a friendly stranger to pet it while it is out with its handler.

Test 3: Appearance and grooming: The dog will welcome being groomed and examined and will permit someone, such as a veterinarian, groomer or friend of the owner, to do so.

Test 4: Out for a walk (walking on a loose lead) : The handler/dog team will take a short "walk" to show that the dog is control while walking on a leash.

Test 5: Walking through a crowd: The dog and handler walk around and pass close to several people (at least three) to demonstrate that the dog can move about politely in pedestrian traffic and is under control in public places.

Test 6: Sit and down on command and staying in place: The dog will respond to the handler's commands to 1) sit, 2) down and will 3) remain in the place commanded by the handler (sit or down position, whichever the handler prefers).

Test 7: Coming when called: The dog will come when called by the handler. The handler will walk 10 feet from the dog, turn to face the dog, and call the dog.

Test 8: Reaction to another dog: To demonstrate that the dog can behave politely around other dogs, two handlers and their dogs approach each other from a distance of about 20 feet, stop, shake hands and exchange pleasantries, and continue on for about 10 feet.

Test 9: Reaction to distraction: To demonstrate the dog is confident when faced with common distracting situations, the evaluator will select and present two distractions. Examples of distractions include dropping a chair, rolling a crate dolly past the dog, having a jogger run in front of the dog, or dropping a crutch or cane.

Test 10: Supervised separation: This test demonstrates that a dog can be left with a trusted person, if necessary, and will maintain training and good manners. Evaluators are encouraged to say something like, "Would you like me to watch your dog?" and then take hold of the dog's leash. The owner will go out of sight for three minutes.

When your dog passes the CGC test, the evaluator will give you the paperwork to send to AKC to request the CGC certificate. If you choose, you may also order a CGC tag for your dog's collar, a patch, leash and scarf acknowledging your dog's success in earning the title of Canine Good citizen.

AKC Community Canine
Advanced CGC

AKC Community Canine extends the skills learned in CGC to the community. AKC Community Canine is the third and most advanced level of the Canine Good Citizen Program. Dogs who pass the AKC Community Canine test are eligible for the "CGCA" (Advanced CGC) title. As with CGC, AKC Community Canine has a 10-step test of skills that dogs must pass to earn the official AKC Community Canine title. This is a title that appears on the dog's title record at AKC. More information at www.akc.org/dogowner/ training/canine_good_citizen/index.cfm

Requirements

To earn the AKC Community Canine title, dogs must meet the following two requirements:

1. Must already have a Canine Good Citizen (CGC) award or title on record at AKC.

2. Must have an AKC number of one of three types (AKC registration number, PAL number, or AKC Canine Partners number). All dogs, including mixed breeds, can get an AKC number. The reason for the AKC number requirement is that this is how we create titles at AKC; we attach the titles to the dog's number. For more information on getting an AKC number, see: http://images.akc.org/cgc/number.pdf

The 10 test skills include:

1.Dog stands, sits or lies down and waits under control while the owner sits at the registration table and fills out paperwork or while the owner sits and has a snack or visits with someone (*e.g.,* at a park).

2. Walks on a loose leash in a natural situation (not in a ring) and does not pull; left and right turn, stop, fast and slow pace

3. Walks on a loose leash through a crowd. This item is tested in a real crowd, not in a ring.

4. Dog walks past distraction dogs present; does not pull.

5. Sit-stay in small group (three other people with dogs). Owners and dogs are in an informal group while owners have a conversation.

6. Dog allows person who is carrying something (*e.g.,*

purse, computer case, backpack) to approach and pet it. "May I pet your dog?" (Item is put on floor/ground before person pets dog)

7. "Leave it." Dog walks by food and follows owner instructions, "Leave it."

8. Down or sit stay (owner's choice) at a distance.

9. Recall with distractions present (coming when called). Handler goes out 20 feet (off center) and calls dog. Dog comes past a distractor to return to handler.

10. Dog enters/exits a doorway or narrow passageway (on leash, with owner) in a controlled manner.

When your dog passes the CGCA test, the evaluator will give you the paperwork to send to AKC to request the CGCA title certificate. You can also order an AKC Community Canine medallion and a CGCA patch.

AKC URBAN CANINE GOOD CITIZEN

AKC Urban CGC is a title in the Canine Good Citizen family of awards and titles that also include AKC S.T.A.R. Puppy, Canine Good Citizen and AKC Community Canine.

AKC Urban CGC requires that the dog demonstrate CGC skills and beyond in an urban setting.

As with Canine Good Citizen, AKC Urban CGC has a 10-step test of skills that dogs must pass to earn the official AKC Urban CGC title. This is a title that appears on the dog's title record at AKC.

All skills in the test are tested on leash. AKC Urban CGC should be administered in a place where there are cars, streets to be crossed, noises, and distractions. This test is administered in the real world; it should not be simulated in a ring at a dog show.

When test items (such as riding on an elevator) are administered in public buildings, the buildings must be dog friendly or evaluators must have permission in advance from the business owners, managers, etc. The goal of AKC Urban CGC is to test the dog's skills in an urban (city) setting.

REQUIREMENTS
To earn the AKC Urban CGC (CGCU) title, dogs must meet the following two requirements:

1. Must already have a Canine Good Citizen (CGC) certificate or title on record at AKC. While the CGC and CGCU may be tested on the same day, the dog owner should request the CGC first. After receiving the CGC certificate, the CGCU can be applied for.

2. Must have an AKC number of one of 3 types (AKC registration number, PAL number, or AKC Canine Partners number). All dogs, including mixed breeds, can get an AKC number. The reason for the AKC number requirement is that this is how we create titles at AKC; we attach the titles to the dog's number. Read more information on getting an AKC number.

The AKC URBAN CGC test items include:

1. Exit/enter doorway with no pulling in dog-friendly buildings. Exit building to start test, additional public buildings items are below.

2. Walk through a crowd on a busy urban sidewalk. People come toward the dog from 1-ft. away. Tolerate distractions (people wearing hats, coats, men, women, etc).

3. Appropriate reaction to city distractions. This includes movement, noises and walking on a variety of surfaces. Examples: Noises: horns, sirens, construction noise, etc. Moving objects: skateboard, bike, carts, person running Surfaces: concrete, grass, grates, plastic tarp, wet sidewalk

4. Crossing street: Stop at corner, stand or sit to wait and cross with no pulling (on leash, with owner). Crosses street under control.

5. Ignore food on sidewalk. (Dropped food, or cups, bags, cans in which food was wrapped).

6. Person walks up and pets the dog. May be carrying an item such as a small dog in a bag, a computer bag, etc. Person does not put the bag down to pet the dog.

7. Public Building (that is dog friendly). Walks under control in building (slick surface, carpeted floor). Down stay (3 min) in lobby or outdoor area, or waits while owner has a meal or snack.

8. Stairs, steps or elevator under control. Steps (at least three - up and down) Elevator (Enters under control, exits, rides under control)

9. Housetrained for apartment, condo, city living. Owner may verify this item. Evaluator may also observe in public buildings, or have observed in training classes.

10. Transportation. Owner's choice depending on owners transportation needs.

Car: Enters/exits, remains under control during the ride. (Crate? Seatbelt?) Subway: Small dog in bag for ride. (large dogs are not always permitted; know and abide by the Transit Policies in your area). Dog friendly: (enters/ exits or allows to be put in/taken out) under control.

To pass the CGCU test, dogs must pass all ten items of the test. When your dog passes the CGCU test, the evaluator will give you the paperwork to send to AKC to request the CGCU title certificate. You can also order an AKC Urban CGC medallion and a CGCU patch.

From the authors: The idea of recognition is strictly up to you. There are some costs involved for title registration. Although it's not the titles and tags that make a wonderful therapy dog, it is nice to know that all your efforts at training and volunteering can earn you some very special recognition.

Chapter 9
Teaching Tricks

"People teach their dogs to sit; it's a trick.
I've been sitting my whole life, and a dog has never looked
at me as though he thought I was tricky."
Mitch Hedberg

Picture Sandy visiting the residents at a nursing home with her beloved Australian shepherd, Rex; Rex gracefully greets every human being and lets them pet on his back and under his ears. As Sandy approaches the courtyard, she notices several residents gathered around the tables. Their eyes light up as they watch Sandy and Rex approach them. With permission, Sandy instructs Rex to show the residents how he can "roll-over", "wipe his eyes" and "take a bow". The residents are fascinated by the performance and clap and cheer for more, which Rex agrees to happily. Needless to say, this therapy team is a big hit among the residents.

Tej happily offers a hand shake

Performing tricks in a safe and controlled manner can add a whole new dimension to your animal assisted activity work. People love to watch pooches perform routines and tricky maneuvers in unison with their handlers. It brings much needed joy and laughter to the residents and your dog gets the entire accolade.

It takes a lot of discipline, dedication, and hard work on your part to make this a reality. Of course safety of the residents, your dog, and yourself should be first and foremost on your mind when you undertake the performance of any trick. You should only demonstrate those tricks that had been practiced before – it is not advisable to experiment with a new tricks during a visit. Although food treats may be used during the training phase, it is our recommendation not to use edible treats during the enactment at the facility. Instead, train your pooch to get excited and demonstrate the tricks to your cheerful voice command.

In this chapter, we will discuss a few fun tricks that are easy to teach and can be supplemented to a typical animal assisted therapy visit.

Things to consider
- Before you start and training, we recommend you consult with your veterinarian to decide on the health of your dog to perform any tricks.
- Always get prior approval from the visiting facility administrator about incorporating tricks in your therapy visits
- During the training, your goal should be to help your dog understand the trick and be successful. Therefore, always use a lot of praise and end on a high note
- Reward your dog to work with you and learn a new trick. This can be food treats, favorite toy, clicker sound, or your verbal praise
- In dog training, reward timing is very important. You should strive to reward the dog the moment he or she does something right

- If your dog is being mischievous, instead of using "No" say "whoops" or "ahh-haa"
- Have a release word like "Done" or "good dog" to help your dog understand when he is under your control and when he has been released
- It is a good idea to have a hand signal (in addition to a verbal cue) for each trick. As your dog advances through the training, you should attempt to use more hand signal and fewer words.
- Your dog should be clean and properly groomed before performing tricks. Be extra careful with his nails while allowing residents to shake hands with your pooch

The Tricks

The step-by-step guidance assume that your dog knows the basic obedience commands "sit", "down", "come" and "stay". Our handy tools include soft yummy treats and canned, spray cheese and a clicker.

Shake Hands – *your dog raises his paw and allows another person to shake his paw.*

1. Start with your dog in a sit position facing you
2. Take a treat in your right hand and bring the hand low to the ground near the dog's right paw
3. Encourage your dog to paw your hand. As he touches your hand, give him the treat, and praise him by saying "Good Shake Hands"
4. Gradually raise the height of your hand until he can raise the paw to his face height.

Roll Over – *your dog rolls sideways on his back from one direction to another*

1. Start with your dog in a **down** position facing you. Kneel down in front of your dog, holding a reward above his head. Make sure he sees the reward in your hand

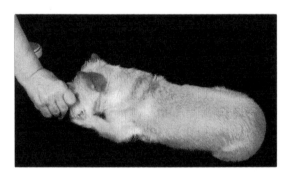

2. Slowly move the treat from his nose towards his shoulder blades and give the command "roll over". The dog will follow the reward and roll on his side

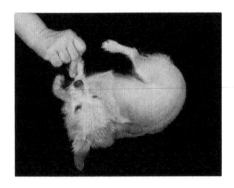

3. Praise him and release the reward. As your dog improves, incorporate a hand signal during the exercise.

Wipe your Eyes – _your dog wipes below his eyes with his paw_

1. Take a piece of scotch tape and stick it to your dog's muzzle below the eyes

2. Instinctively he will try to get the tape off his muzzle by using his paw

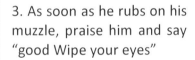

3. As soon as he rubs on his muzzle, praise him and say "good Wipe your eyes"

4. As the dog advances, incorporate a hand signal to replace the verbal cue

Back Up (like a truck) – your dog backs up in a straight line away from you

1. Start with the dog in a **stand** position in front of you in a hallway or corridor. Use a confined area so that the dog does not have the opportunity to turn but can only go forwards or backwards.

Use an x-pen and garage door to create a confined space.

2. Slowly take a few steps towards the dog. When he takes one step backwards, click and treat. For some dogs, a couple of steps in their direction work best but for other dogs, a slight lean into the dog is more effective.

3. Continue to reinforce your dog for taking a step backwards. Gradually continue moving toward your dog until he has taken more than one step backwards. Reinforce him for multiple steps.

4. Once he understands that backing up is a way to earn treats, say the cue "back up" before moving toward him. Look at your dog's tail rather than his eyes as you step towards him

5. Add the cue "be a truck". As the dog is backing up, the handler makes the "beep, beep, beep" sound of a truck backing up.

Spin/Twist – your dog spins a full circle, counter-clockwise (spin) or clockwise (twist)

1. Start with your dog in sit or stand position facing you.

2. Using the spray cheese can as a pointer or long soft treat, lure your dog in a large counter-clockwise circle while using the que "spin"

3. Reward him with a squirt of cheese or a piece of treat once he completes a full circle

4. Repeat the above steps in clockwise direction and use the command "twist"

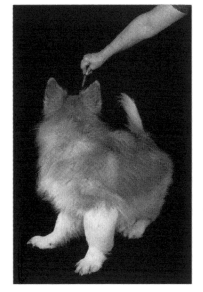

5. As the dog improves, incorporate hand signals to replace the verbal cue

Weave between legs – _your dog crosses back and forth between your legs as you walk_

1. Start with your dog standing at your left side (heel position). Have several small tasty treats in both hands

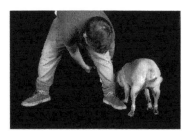

2. Take a big step with your right foot and lower your right hand between your legs. Give him the verbal cue "weave"

3. The dog will smell the treat in your right hand and cross between your legs. As soon as he crosses your legs, reward him with the treat from your right hand

4. Now take a big step with your left foot and lower your left hand between your legs while giving the verbal cue "weave"

5. As soon as he crosses your legs, reward him with the treat from your left hand. Repeat the steps.

6. As your dog advances, incorporate a hand signal to replace the verbal cue

**Take a Bow** – _your dog bows by keeping his hind legs upright and front legs touching the floor_

1. Have the dog start from a stand position

2. Have a treat in your right hand and stand to the right side of the dog

3. Place your left hand under the dog's body and keep his back legs upright

4. Place your right hand with the treat on the floor in front of the dog's nose

5. As the dog goes to take the treat from your right hand, his elbows will touch the floor. Release the treat and praise him with "Good Take a Bow"

6. As he advances, incorporate a hand signal to replace the verbal cue

Chapter 10
Knowing When to Quit

"Dogs have always been here; but we humans are just now discovering ways to tap into their phenomenal gifts. We've begun that process, and now it's time to discover whether what we ask of them measures up to what each individual dog is designed to give. Humans have a history of using natural resources indiscriminately, then feeling sorry afterward. Our obligation now is to serve as our dog's advocate, appreciating them for just who and what they are, and not projecting our images of success onto them. That's exactly what our dogs do for us. Their best gifts are the looks that say "I love you, man. You're just right" Our obligation is to return the gift."

-Kris Butler,
from Therapy Dogs Today: Their Gifts, Our Obligation

Questions to ask when deciding to retire your dog from therapy work

- Is your dog exhibiting tiredness during visits

- Is your dog no longer excited about going on visits

- Is your dog still healthy enough to continue therapy work

- Is your dog uncomfortable with the constant petting from strangers

- Has your dog lost his enthusiasm for meeting and greeting strangers

- Is your dog physically capable of walking for extended periods

> To ask *"What can I learn from you?"* acknowledges that all of us – including animals-serve at one time or another as teachers for each other.
>
> *This humble question reminds us that we are, all of us, students of life; learning and growth are not phases we pass through on our way to adulthood, but the constant companions of our daily life.*
>
> *When we are willing to ask this most fundamental of questions, something profound shifts inside of us, creating an awareness that wherever we look, there are teachers bearing truths great and small for our lives."*
>
> Suzanne Clothier
> from
> Bones Would Rain
> from the Sky

As the use of dogs in Animal Assisted Intervention programs becomes more and more popular, it is vitally important that handlers remember that they are partners with their dog and as such, must serve as their advocate. You volunteered for this job, your dog didn't! Never push him to do something that makes him uncomfortable. There may be a situation, a circumstance or a person that is "just not for him". Don't push! Advocate. Your dog is doing all he can to try to please you. Don't stretch his abilities. Your visits should build your relationship with your dog, not hinder it. Establish good communication with your dog. Find situations that are comfortable for him and stay within the boundaries the dog sets for your visits. After each visit, take a minute to ask yourself "Did my dog enjoy the visit as much as I did?" Don't let your desire to serve overshadow your dog's needs. If your dog becomes anxious or afraid, the potential for danger increases.

So ask yourself, is this the right job for this dog??? If so, move forward full steam! If you have any hesitation about your answer, put your dog's needs first. If therapy work is not for him, so be it! Don't be disappointed. You have a wonderful dog with whom you have built an enviable relationship. Relax and enjoy the extra special therapy he provides to you.

Ginny Belle

at her retirement party

Photo by Tom Gaffney

My dog , Ginny Belle, was a Corgi mix with short legs and an extra long body. From the age of one when she was certified, she loved her visits and always looked forward to them. As she aged, it got harder for those stubby legs to carry her around the huge facility she had served for many years. Her mind and body were still sharp, strong and eager to serve, but her little legs just couldn't keep up. The solution? A dog stroller. Ginny absolutely loved her stroller. It made her high enough for the patients to easily reach her and she could comfortably continue to enjoy her visits. The residents loved watching her move through the facility on four wheels. She was able to continue her visits into her 17th year. When she retired, we had a big celebration at the facility with all the people she loved so much.

Lee

If you are lucky enough to enjoy years together as a therapy team, the day will come when you will have to think about retiring the dog. You may start to notice your dog slowing down during his walks through the facility. He may grow disinterested in the constant barrage of new people reaching out to pet him. Again, don't push. Be thankful for the wonderful time you have spent together, the many hours you have shared bringing joy to others. Do the right thing for your dog... retire.

"My face may be white but my heart is pure gold.
There is no shame is growing old.
Author Unknown

Abby
March 1, 2000-May 24, 2015
Animal Assisted Activity Dog
for 12 years

Beaucoup Lagniappe
(Lots more extras!)

Yaeger

My son, Matt, had just moved into his first apartment and

Yeager and Matt

wanted a canine companion . His girlfriend decided she would give him a puppy for Valentine's Day. Together, they went to the area shelter to see what they could find. The minute Matt saw Yaeger, he fell in love with him. He looked at all of the dogs there but kept coming back to Yaeger, a sandy colored Staffordshire bull terrier mix with a white chest and white paws and very, very handsome! The staff estimated that he was approximately seven months to a year old. He had been found as a stray and brought into the shelter showing signs of abuse. His sad eyes kept tugging at Matt's heart. Knowing that I would have to help take care of Yaeger, Matt felt obliged to inform me that his prospective new pet was a "pit bull". I immediately said "no way . . . those dogs are very dangerous!" He pleaded with me to return with him the next day to the SPCA to meet Yaeger and to see how precious he was. I agreed knowing that I would find another more suitable pet for my son. I suggested a couple of dogs but Matt insisted on Yaeger. I spoke to the agency supervisor expressing my concerns about this breed. She assured me that pitbulls were very gentle and sweet dogs and that their bad reputation was not their fault but that of their owners who raised them to be aggressive. She confessed that she owned two pitties of her own and they were the sweetest, most gentle dogs, especially with children.

I reluctantly agreed to the adoption but with strict instructions that my son take him to obedience school for proper training.

Once Matt brought Yaeger to his apartment the results of the previous abuse became much more apparent. Yagi was very skittish, cowering to loud noises like the rustling of a garbage bag, and hiding at the crisp sound of shaking laundry before being folded. Today, he still goes into another room when I fold clothes. He rarely barked. It was not until he spent time with my daughter's three dogs that he joined in with their barking. Because he was still a pup he loved to chew . . . on everything and anything! He chewed a couple of Matt's television remotes, more than one pair of his favorite and expensive sneakers, furniture, and even light bulbs!! Through thick and thin, Matt and Yagi became best friends. He was Matt's companion when visiting family, friends, his work place and, of course, his bed mate. He was described as a "bed hog". Once he found the perfect spot on the bed there was no moving him! Matt truly loved his best friend.

Our grandchild was a dog! We would babysit when needed and soon enough we began spoiling him as grandparents do best. He greeted every visitor with a few licks, yet was very protective of us when strangers approached. My husband always shared a bit of his meals with Yagi and treats were plentiful. We, too, truly loved our canine "grandson".

In April of 2006, our son, Matt, was tragically killed in a car accident. Yaeger sensed our immense grief as well as his own and stayed close to us offering us many kisses and snuggles. He brought us well-needed comfort. Our therapy became daily long walks with Yaeger and he was more than happy to oblige. In memory of our son, several of Matt's friends, as well as our friends and family, helped us erect a memory garden. I had purchased a resin boy cherub to place in it. As I unwrapped the angel Yaeger walked over to it and very curiously sniffed it for almost a minute. His deep interest took me by surprise and brought tears to my eyes because I truly believe he sensed a connection to it! We realized how blessed we were to now have Matt's loving and cherished companion as a permanent part of our family.

Over the next 4 years Yaeger continued to bring us immense happiness and comfort. As I began to heal I wanted to share Yaeger with others because he knew what to do to make others smile. I noticed an article in the newspaper about the Visiting Pet Program. I knew that Yaeger was the perfect candidate! He successfully passed the evaluation and soon began "bringing love and leaving smiles".

He is such a natural therapy pet. On our visits, he immediately positions himself next to the patients and greets them with smiles and even a few kisses. In turn, he thoroughly enjoys being the center of attention and the recipient of great affection. He especially enjoys visiting with the children and their families making sure he greets everyone in the room and not leaving until he is shown affection in return.

On Valentine's Day of 2015, Yagi turned 12 years old. He has had some health problems and has slowed down somewhat. Yet, he continues to look forward to outings, especially to his monthly hospital visits where he has done his therapy work for the last five years. Hopefully, there will be a few more of visits.

Yaeger and Tere Walsh

Today, Yagi continues to be my dear and constant companion. In February of 2010 my husband died suddenly at the age of 54. Once again, my beloved pet was there for me and gave me so much needed love and comfort. Getting out of bed was so difficult but having to care for Yaeger gave me purpose and saved my life. He greeted me when I got home to an otherwise empty house. He snuggled with me during my lowest moments and smothered me with kisses. He continued to be my loyal walking buddy during our much lonelier therapeutic walks. We will continue to take care of each other as best friends do. This Valentine's Day pup is a rescue dog but I often ask myself "Who saved Who?".

Tere Walsh
Covington, LA

Olive Oyl

When we lost our 17 year old dog, my wife, Cathy, and I didn't rush to get another dog. Our loss was a great one and it took us some time to heal. At that time, I traveled frequently for my job. One day, my work took me to the Lafourche Animal Shelter in Thibodeaux, Louisiana. Before leaving the house, I casually asked my wife if she wanted me to pick out a dog while I was there. Her response was "yes, a small female".

When I entered the shelter, I was overwhelmed by the wide variety of dogs available for adoption. In an effort to narrow my search, I asked the adoption counselor if she happened to have a small, female dog. Of course she did!

I entered the kennel and spotted a tiny, black ball of fur. As soon as she saw me, her tail started wagging furiously and she started jumping all over the kennel. It was love at first sight for both of us. I took her outside for a few minutes and I knew this pup was coming home with me. It's hard to say if we rescued "Olive Oyl" or if she rescued us.

Years later, our son was severely injured in an accident. We spent many long hours in the hospital by his bed side. We frequently noticed dogs visiting patients on the floors and in the rehabilitation unit. The dogs brought so much joy to the patients and really brightened the day of everyone whose paths they crossed. Knowing Olive's outgoing personality and gentle nature, Cathy casually mentioned "you and Olive should do that". So we did!

We became part of the Visiting Pet Program in New Orleans. Olive loves her work, especially with the kids at Children's Hospital and several summer camps for children with special needs. There are always requests for a special visit from Olive at the nursing homes she frequents. When we arrive at our visits, Olive starts whining to get out of the car before I've even finished parking.

Mike Azarello and Olive Oyl

That little, black, wagging ball of fur has a whole lot of love to give. Her muzzle is a little grey now but she is still hard at work spreading the happiness only four paws can bring.

Mike Azzarello
Metairie, LA

Maggie

I decided I wanted to work with a therapy dog when my mom, diagnosed with brain cancer, was in and out of the hospital for over a year. A group would come visit with small animals, mostly dogs, and they brought back a part of her life that she was losing. I would take time off from work to be at the hospital so I could make sure that she was able to meet and love all of the animals. She, and I, loved it! My only sister had a prolonged progressive illness for about 3 years and was also frequently in the hospital. She, too, loved the animal visits. It felt like home for a few minutes. I decided that when I retired

Pat Egers and Maggie

from my demanding job, I would adopt a rescue dog and bring joy to patents or residents. It was my overriding goal for my new life.

How Maggie and I found each other seems like kismet. In talking with my new neighbors about my upcoming retirement they mentioned that they had friends in Georgia who rescued dogs, goats and horses on their farm. If I agreed, they would send me photos of dogs that seem to be candidates for therapy work. The first photo sent me was of Maggie—a glamour shot. My heart melted. They rescued her from a shelter that was shutting off power over the holidays! Maggie was pregnant and the shelter was begging for help.

Maggie went to the farm and delivered 10 healthy puppies on New Year's Day 2010! One of her rescuers, a retired mid-wife, told me that Mags was a wonderful mother. Both women agreed that Maggie was a special dog and they predicted she had the personality and soul to give her love to others in therapy work.

I had a brief debate with myself. I live in post-Katrina New Orleans. I wanted a small dog that would make evacuation easier. Maggie was 45 pounds. Then, I looked at her soulful eyes in the pictures. My co-workers fell in love with her, too, and I knew we were meant for each other. I agreed to adopt her, and when we met for the first time it was instant love! The two women who rescued her drove her to New Orleans, simultaneously smiling and crying. I still send updates to them as they are a part of Maggie's successful therapy career.

I received information on the Visiting Pet Program in New Orleans and was so anxious to start that I went to the orientation meeting too early! You must have the dog for six months before you can apply for evaluations!! In the meantime, we did all the prep work... went to obedience school, doggy day care and just got to know each other. Those who met Maggie noticed her loving qualities. When we were eligible to apply to the Visiting Pet Program, I was very nervous at the pet-handler evaluation. What if we didn't pass? Thankfully, all the prep work paid off and we passed our evaluation.

My Maggie loves her therapy visits. We visit a nursing home monthly and recently began going to Children's Hospital of New Orleans During her visits, Maggie walks down the halls with her tail wagging looking for people to love. I was so surprised to see the number of nurses, doctors, staff, and parents who get down on the floor to pet her. She provides comfort and rejuvenation to the staff as well as patients. The nursing home, especially, reminds me of the importance of touch. Sometimes a resident will close his eyes and gently stroke through her soft fur soaking in all the love she has to offer. It brings a smile to my face just thinking about it.

On our daily walks, Maggie and I pass a residence for people with dementia. Maggie, totally on her own, sensed their need for her. With the approval of personnel, Maggie now visits eager residents on the front porch. They love her and look forward to her daily visits.

Each semester, we also participate in a Charity School of Nursing class on "Health and Illness". I give a presentation on animals as an alternative therapy used in medicine while Maggie shares her special brand of caring as she walks along the rows of nursing students. That presentation expanded to visiting the nursing students during final exam week to help the nervous students relax during exams. Maggie handles the varied emotional reactions with her usual canine understanding. She is a champion psychotherapist. I marvel at her intuitive understanding of what someone needs from her.

After a visit Maggie is generally very tired, a good tired. So am I. Seeing the smiles on the faces means a lot to me.

I am reminded of how Maggie's predecessors helped my family and me cope during our tough times.

My rescued dog, Maggie, is a very special girl and we were lucky to find each other. She makes my life, and the lives of all those she touches, a little bit better.

Patricia Egers
New Orleans, LA

A Rescuers Tale

What happens to that 10 pound precious pedigreed puppy that turns into an unwanted, neglected, 80 pound dog? The answer...Boxer Rescue, or Golden Rescue, or Sheltie or Greyhound or Lab or Dalmatian...you get the picture.

My name is Connie Back and I am the founder and director of Louisiana Boxer Rescue, a 501c3 organization dedicated to the rehabilitation and safe rehoming of my favorite breed, the Boxer. Our organization rehomes approximately 100-135 Boxers a year. We also, from time to time, find ourselves with Boxer mixes that charm their way into our foster homes.

Patiently waiting

As a rescue organization, we are tasked with finding foster homes, attending to medical needs, dealing with behavior issues, screening adoption applicants, creating and attending fundraisers, and facing the daily realization that we cannot save them all. It's a lot for a small group of dedicated volunteers but the rewards are ten fold! When I walk into a shelter and see a scared, usually malnourished, sometimes abused Boxer cringing, shivering and cowering in a corner, it breaks my heart. Then, I have the great pleasure of walking the dog out of the shelter that initially saved him and driving him away to a new beginning. That is the best feeling I have ever had. Watching him thrive and ultimately go to a home with a new family... that's the icing on the cake.

Rescue work takes a lot of commitment and is almost impossible to walk away from once you are involved. I know. I have been doing it for more than 20 years now. I've missed many family events, had to cancel planned vacations and even evacuated for Hurricane Katrina with 28 dogs! Most of our volunteers work full time, have families, outside activities and still have to find the time to care for their foster. It is easy to understand how much we cherish our foster homes. I personally house anywhere from 8-15 fosters at a time; most homes foster one or two.

Prior to adoption, our Boxers are thoroughly health checked, spayed/neutered, have their teeth cleaned, treated for heartworms, if necessary, and are temperament tested. The foster homes work on crate and potty training, basic commands like sit, stay and come as well as good manners. Once a rescue Boxer is adopted, he may go on to do a variety of activities. The new family may choose to have just a happy family pet or they may go on to performance work such as obedience, agility, tracking, search and rescue, or a number of other sports.... and yes....THERAPY DOG. Several of my dogs and I have been very active with the local animal assisted therapy group for many, many years. My experience with the group has taught me how to evaluate our rescue dogs that may have real potential for therapy work.

For example, there was Oban. He was rescued from a dead end street in a rural area, was being offered for sale at a garage sale! Boxer Rescue volunteers in Baton Rouge picked him up and brought him to New Orleans. He was in typical abandoned dog shape... thin and infected with heartworms. With some TLC in rescue, Oban was adopted

Oban
Photo by Joy Sturtevant

by a wonderful woman who was mesmerized by his big ears.

She enrolled him in obedience and agility classes. Oban excelled at both. Looking for more adventures for Oban, his new owner tested him for the area animal assisted therapy program. Oban excelled at that, too! He seemed like a natural. He loved the children at the Reading to Rover events where he could just lie on the carpet and have children stroke him as they read. When visiting the nursing homes, Oban's calmness was contagious. The elderly eagerly anticipated his monthly visits. Oban was always happy to oblige.

Then there was Benny. **He was soooo skinny that his**

head looked enormous. He had tapeworms and heartworms. Oban's future owner offered to foster Benny for a little while to give him a comfortable home while he regained his health. After a more intensive veterinary exam, poor Benny was determined to have had a broken leg that had not healed correctly, some metal that looked like a sewing machine needle in his upper right front shoulder area and was riddled with shotgun pellets. What a mess! Needless to say, he never left that foster home!

Benny

Through all of his hardships, Benny was still a real lover. He's never met a dog or human he doesn't love and he is sure they love him back. He became a member of the Visiting Pet Program and made it his mission in life to bring love to everyone. Whether it's listening to a child read a book or staring intently into the eyes of an older adult recounting stories of a dog he had many years ago, Benny never waivers from his goal of bringing a smile to everyone he meets.

Through the joys and hardships, rescue is my mission in life. It is stories like Benny's and Oban's that keep me going.

Connie Back
River Ridge, LA

Penny

My Greyhound, Penny, and I had been doing nursing home visits and school presentations for several years. Penny was a retired racer, adopted through "It's a Grey Area" Greyhound adoptions. She was a white brindle with what looked like a heart on her side. Her racing name was Visions of Heart. Very appropriate.

When I attended orientation for the Visiting Pet Program, I remember them telling us to 'expect the unexpected on a visit'. That wasn't just lip service. The unexpected has happened to me several times.

One memorable occasion was a Tuesday morning as I was getting ready to make an animal assisted therapy visit with my Penny. I was a little apprehensive that morning because we were going to make our first visit in the Chemotherapy Treatment Center. I didn't have any doubts about my dog. I just wanted to make sure I was doing the right thing and didn't know what to expect.

As we got out of the car in the parking garage, a couple was eagerly waiting for us. Apparently, they saw Penny in the back seat of my car as we drove up. They were mesmerized by her and anxious to meet her. Penny won their hearts immediately. I attempted to explain our program and the benefits of animal assisted therapy to the couple but I honestly don't think they heard a word I said. Before I knew it, they were both on their knees, hugging and loving on Penny. It seemed like we were there forever. Eventually they explained they were grief stricken and were on their way to visit a relative in the Critical Care Unit, probably for the last time. The couple thanked me and told me how much their time with Penny meant to them. That was our first therapy visit in a hospital parking garage! That exchange deeply touched my heart.

While walking down the hallway in the Chemotherapy Treatment Center, we were stopped by two nurses. They immediately connected with Penny. One of the nurses exclaimed that Penny was also her name! That made me feel good and gave me the extra confidence needed to enter the treatment center.

Penny

What a reception we received! The patients were surprised to see a dog in the treatment center. The smiles that came across their faces told me that this was going to be a very positive experience. As I approached each patient, I asked if they would like a visit from Penny. The majority eagerly said yes. They told me about their pet(s) and had many questions about Penny, Greyhounds in general and about animal assisted therapy. Several of them wanted to pet her; some wanted to take her home! For many of the patients, this was their first experience meeting a Greyhound. A few patients expressed that did not care for dogs, so we stood back and simply offered a "good morning" greeting which usually brought on a positive response. Our little adventure brightened up the day of both patients and staff.

As soon as we got to the car, I rewarded Penny with a special treat. The ride home only took fifteen minutes and but she slept all the way! Being the center of attention can be quite exhausting!

At our next hospital visit, the nurses couldn't wait to tell me that after Penny's last visit, the patients started interacting and showing each other photos of their pets. The usually quiet treatment center made up of patients sleeping, reading or watching TV was turned into a lively facility with people sharing stories and photos of their much -loved animals. My rescued Greyhound did that!

Barbara Hyland
Kenner, LA

The Canine "Doc"

It was shortly before closing my veterinary clinic for the day when my receptionist came to me and said there was a person at the front desk who wanted to euthanize his dog. It wasn't unusual to have someone come in like that at the very end of the day, not wanting their dog to suffer through another night. In this case, however, my receptionist quickly informed me that the owner of the animal was not a client of mine and that there was nothing wrong with the dog. In fact, the dog was just a puppy.

The puppy was brought into the exam room. When I walked into the room to talk to the client, what do I see at the end of the leash? A black, standard Poodle about 5 months old, full of energy and enthusiasm. The dog, with tongue hanging out and tail wagging constantly, kept lunging forward to greet me. Each time he lunged, he pulled so hard that, when he got to the end of his leash, he would fall over on his side. That didn't stop him. He'd just get up and do it again!

After thoroughly examining the dog and finding nothing medically wrong with him, I determined the dog's only issue was that he was a happy puppy. The owner told me stories of how the dog was "out of control", "un-trainable", and most importantly, "destructive"!!! I started thinking to myself that this guy must have come home that night and found something of great value to him torn to shreds across the floor of his house. I started talking with the gentleman about training his dog but he was not interested in my advice at all. His only goal was to put the dog to sleep. Saying he didn't want to be there for the euthanization procedure, he walked out of the clinic, got in his car and drove off.

Mike, one of my assistants who has worked with me for the last 23 years, looked at me and then looked at the dog and said "Can I have him?" Mike came up with the name

"Doc" for the energetic Poodle. Over the next few months, with some training, love and attention, "Doc" turned into fabulous canine companion.

A few years later, a client of mine started talking about therapy dog programs. I had been part of a small group when I was in vet school. However, at the time, there was no one in New Orleans doing therapy visits at our local Children's Hospital. I spoke to another client who was doing her residency in child psychology at Children's Hospital of New Orleans. She was able to open some doors for us and we were able to start a very informal therapy dog program.

At the time, I had a Jack Russell Terrier named Tammy, who was great with kids. My client who was participating with me had Golden Retrievers. After a few weeks of visiting, Tammy was pulled from the program for snapping at one of the doctors (she was a Jack Russell after all!) After the horror of that visit, but undaunted in my efforts to bring dogs to hospitalized kids, I talked to Mike about possibly bringing Doc to visit the kids. Mike agreed to let me borrow Doc.

Doc

On his very first visit, Doc acted like he had done therapy work his whole life. He would gently place his two front paws on the bedrail and either give a high 5 or a generous lick to the children as they sat on their bed. Anytime a child approached him, he would sit and enjoy the attention given to him. It was always amazing to watch him spread pure joy to those kids.

I am thankful to God for bringing Dog to my veterinary clinic on that Thursday afternoon. Doc knew he had a purpose to fulfill in his second chance at life. It was an honor for me to be part of Doc's life and a treat to witness him work his magic on the sick children at the hospital.

Scott Abadie, DVM
River Ridge, LA

Kansas

When I adopted my first Greyhound in 1998 I had never even heard of "pet therapy". That first Greyhound, Kansas, just happened to be the shy, timid type. My goal for her was to make her as comfortable and confident as possible. As I was going through the process to help her become all she could be, I was introduced to the concept of animal assisted therapy and animal assisted activities. As luck would have it, the training and socializing we were working on to build her confidence was also exactly what we needed to prepare her to become a therapy dog.

Based on my experience, I can say that that if you are starting with a shy dog, it is impossible to put a real time frame on your efforts. It can take at least 6 to 12 months of consistent, ongoing work to help your dog become relaxed, confident and self-assured. As an owner of one of these special dogs, I soon learned that as a human and the dog's handler, I had to have the right attitude. Having the attitude of being a calm, confident and skillful handler will transfer right down the leash to the dog.

I live in an urban area. In the beginning, Kansas was fearful of buses, garbage trucks, motorcycles, and anything with sirens, making it very difficult to simply walk down the block with her. My approach with Kansas was to slowly take her to as many places as possible and progressively introduce her to different sights and sounds. We started at the opposite end of the block from the main thoroughfare. Over several weeks, we gradually worked our way closer to the active area. I soon realized that as her handler, I must remain relaxed and in-charge. Since Kansas was already fearful, I didn't want her to feed off any of my negative energy. I learned to shrug a lot and say out loud "it's only a bus, an ambulance, a garbage truck". This basic work of confidence building had to be done. How else could I walk her if I didn't help her get past these fears?

When I had trouble keeping my mind and thoughts peaceful and tranquil, I found out that it helped to sing a song in my head, however silly the song might be. I always sang *Ninety-Nine Bottles of Beer on the Wall*. It is a long song and kept my mind busy remembering the lyrics and did not allow any nervous thoughts to enter my mind.

Now, you may be thinking "I want to do therapy work with my dog. Who cares about the traffic outside?" If your rescued dog has these or similar issues, by going through this process together, you are building a trusting relationship. With a dog that lacks confidence, you want him, in the beginning, to develop trust in you so that he knows he can depend on you to make decisions and you will let him know what to do next. This type of exercise can be done with anything that instills fear. It helps to start out a distance from the scary thing and slowly work closer and closer towards it over time. Having patience is the key to success. Let the dog move at his chosen pace to build his confidence.

Kansas and Claire Sommers
Photo by Tom Gaffney

Other great ways to build a bond and enhance a trusting relationship are by taking obedience and agility for fun classes. Kansas and I kept taking obedience classes over and over again. After each 6 week session, she visibly became more confident. In the beginning, I would be hesitant to let others invade her space or pet her. As we continued to take classes, Kansas became much more calm; my girl made lots of friends with the other dog owners whom she met every week. This allowed her to build confidence in dealing with different people.

Frequently, when we learned something new in training class, Kansas would have trouble with it in the beginning. It was important for me to not push her to the point that she would shut down and now participate. I wanted to keep the classes a fun place. So, we would go home and practice the commands repeatedly. Since our home was her comfort zone, I would practice every night at home with her. The more things you can do to help your dog learn, the more self-assured he will become. Your dog will look to you for guidance. It's as if he is asking "what do you want me to do next?" That is a wonderful thing to watch happen.

During the training classes, Kansas taught me a lot. I learned how to take a deep breath when she was not performing perfectly, sing in my head, to celebrate the small successes, and to always end on a high note. Sometimes, it helped us to go back to basics and work on the simple exercises she knew so well. The goal of these training classes is not to turn the dog into an obedience champion but to help build a strong bond between a handler and his rescued dog.

While working with Kansas and adding the goal of her becoming a therapy pet, I learned one of the best "cues" for our therapy visits—"Say Hi". Since Kansas was originally fearful of anyone petting her, I started this lesson at home. Again, she was learning new things in her comfort zone. I started doing this with myself at first. Whenever I came home, instead of calling her by name, I would use the words "Say Hi". After this, I would sporadically say the words "Say Hi" and she would come to me for petting.

Once I felt she was getting the idea of "Say Hi", I started practicing the new skill with people who came to our house. I leashed her and would walk up to our visiting friend using the words "Say Hi". My visiting friends were pre -instructed to do appropriate, low key, brief petting. If Kansas wanted to stay and get more attention, that was wonderful.   It was her choice. Once she had gotten comfortable with "Say Hi" at home, we practiced it at obedience or agility class and then in parks and public places. Teaching "Say Hi" lets your dog know exactly what you want them to do when they meet someone. It also lets the dog know that you are telling them this person is okay to greet.   Dogs with an underlying timid or fearful personality need and want this kind of direction from their human handler.

All the hard work paid off. Kansas became an amazing therapy dog and served many years with the Visiting Pet Program in New Orleans. I used these same methods with two other rescued dogs, both with great success. Over the years, I learned that the key to success is to have patience, enjoy small successes and build on each small achievement. This will help an unsure rescued dog be the most relaxed and confident pet for therapy work.

Claire Sommers
New Orleans, LA

Epilogue

Licensed Clinical Social Worker Sharon Henry has been in practice for 30 years. She shares her skills with grieving pet owners as a pet bereavement counselor. She has written poetry for many years. "Surely" was inspired by her work with pet owners. "It really devastates people when a pet dies or has to be euthanized. It's very gratifying and satisfying to help people with their grief, and it gives me great joy to help people during their difficult time. I think because I feel people's losses so deeply myself, that informed my choice of words and motivated me to write this poem."

Marigny with Sharon Henry

"Surely"

Surely a star danced in Heaven the day your dog was born.
Surely daffodils perked and Gabriel blew his horn.
Sure they knew without a doubt,
That she was truly worth shouting about!
Surely a star dimmed in Heaven, on the day your dog died.
Surely daffodils bowed and loved ones cried.
Surely they knew without a doubt,
That she'd be missed 'round and about.
Surely with each breath of Spring, and each song's refrain,
Surely we'll see her at Home,
Dancing with the stars once again.

Sharon Henry, LCSW
Metairie, LA

Fact Sheet:
Pet overpopulation in the United States

(source:aspca.org, August 2015)

- There are about 13,600 independent community animal shelters in the United States
- Each year, approximately 3.9 million dogs enter animal shelters nationwide
- Each year, approximately 1.2 million dogs are euthanized
- Each year, approximately 1.4 million dogs are adopted from United States animal shelters
- It is estimated that 70-80 million dogs are owned in the United States. Approximately 37-48% of all households in the United States have a dog
- The most common reasons people relinquish or give away their dogs is because
  i. their place of residence does not allow pets
  ii. not enough time
  iii. divorce
  iv. death in the family
  v. behavior issues
- The cost of spaying or neutering a pet is less than the cost of raising puppies for a year. Only 10% of the animals received by shelters have been spayed or neutered. About 83% of pet dogs are spayed or neutered

(https://www.aspca.org/about-us/faq/pet-statistic)

Resources

National Animal Assisted Therapy Groups

Pet Partners (formerly Delta Society)
875 124th Ave NE #101
Bellevue, WA 98005-2531
425-679-5530
volunteering@petpartners.org
petpartners.org

Therapy Dogs Inc.
P.O. Box 20227
Cheyenne, WY 82003
877-843-7364
therapydogsinc@qwestoffice.net
therapydogs.com

Therapy Dog International
88 Bartley Road
Flanders, NJ 07836
973-252-9800
tdi@gti.net
tdi-dog.org

Love on a Leash
P.O. Box 4548
Oceanside, CA 92052-4548
(760) 740-2326
info@loveonaleash.org
loveonaleash.org

The Bright & Beautiful Therapy Dogs, Inc.
80 Powder Mill Road
Morris Plains, New Jersey
(888) 738-5770
info@golden-dogs.org
golden-dogs.org

Paws For Friendship, Inc.
P O Box 341378
Tampa, FL 33694
(813) 961-2822
jenniesmom@pawsforfriendshipinc.org
pawsforfriendshipinc.org

Book Resources and Recommended Authors

Dogwise
403 S. Mission St.
Wenatchee, WA 98801
1-800-776-2665 or (509) 663-9115
Dogwise.com

Kris Butler
American Dog Obedience Center, LLC
Funpuddle Publishing Associates
Norman, Oklahoma
405-364-7650
kris@dogprograms.com

Suzanne Clothier
Elemental Animal, Inc.
PO Box 105, St Johnsville,
NY 13452
1-800-7-FLY-DOG or 518 568 3325
info@suzanneclothier.com
suzanneclothier.com

Kathy Diamond Davis
4425 NW 52nd Street
Oklahoma, OK 73112-2115
(405) 947-5413
KDiamondD@aol.com

Ann Howie
Human-Animal Solutions
Olympia, Washington
(360) 493-2586
HumanAnimalSolutions@comcast.net
Humananimalsolutions.com

Patricia McConnell, PhD
McConnell Publishing, Ltd.
1039 Mills Street
Black Earth, WI 53515
(608) 767-2435
patriciamcconnell.com

United Kennel Club
100 East Kilgore Rd.
Kalamazoo, MI 49001-5598
(616)343-9020
Fax: (616)343-7037
www.ukcdogs.com

North American Dog Agility Council
HCR 2, Box 277
St. Maries, Idaho 83861
(208)689-3803
www.nadac.com

Australian Shepherd Club of America
(all breeds and mix breeds welcome)
6091 E. State Hwy 21,
Bryan TX 77808
(979) 778-1082
registrar@asca.org
www.asca.org

Teacup Dogs Agility Association
P.O. Box 48
Waterford, OH 45786
740-749-3597
http://k9tdaa.com

K9 Nose Work
7510 Sunset Blvd #1180
Los Angeles, CA 90046
323.656.1200
info@k9nosework.com

National Association of Canine Scent Work (NACSW) - official
sanctioning and organizing body for the sport of K9 Nose Work.
http://www.nacsw.net/home

Barn Hunt Association, LLC
barnhunt.com
https://www.facebook.com/pages/Barn-Hunt

Other Resources

American Kennel Club (AKC)
8051 Acro Corporate Drive, Suite 100
Raleigh, NC 27617
919-233-9767
akc.org

American Society for the Prevention of Cruelty to Animals (ASPCA)
424 E. 92nd St
New York, NY 10128-6804
(212) 876-7700
publicinformation@aspca.org
aspca.org

Dog Play website
http://www.dogplay.com/Activities/Therapy/index.html#overview

The Humane Society of the United States
2100 L St., NW
Washington, D.C. 20037
202-452-1100 or 866-720-2676
humanesociety.org

Therapy Dog Information website
http://www.therapydoginfo.net/

Dog Sport Organizations

United States Dog Agility Association, Inc.
P.O. Box 850955
Richardson, TX 75085-0955
info@usdaa.com
(972)231-9700
Fax: (214)503-0161
www.USDAA.com

Canine Performance Events
P.O. Box 805
South Lyon, MI 48178
cpe@charter.net
www.k9cpe.com

Acknowledgments

Lee: Since 1982, my wonderful husband, Tom, has been by my side, encouraging even the craziest idea I might have had. He has tolerated many animal adoptions; too many to count. He loved them all and they adored him. He holds the household together so that I can devote time to my passions. He is my inspiration and my rock. And to the mentors who have been with me on this journey: Edye Conkerton, Alison Cook, Joyce Kleinfeldt, and Jim Tedford, I thank them all for sharing their time and talents to help me develop my animal assisted therapy knowledge and skills

*Molly listens attentively
as a resident plays the piano*

Malay: My love for dogs began at a very early age, when my grandfather asked me to bottle feed six new-born German Shepherd puppies in our home back in India. Over the years, I have been fascinated by the love, adoration, and loyalty a dog can bestow upon a human being. I have also been fortunate to know and learn from the extremely dedicated volunteers of Gulf South Golden Retriever rescue, who introduced me to the world of dog rescue, rehabilitation and adoption. I thank all the two-and-four legged personalities who have influenced, nurtured and guided me in the world of dog rescue and animal assisted therapy work.

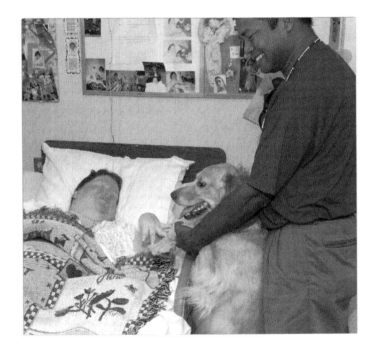

Mita and Malay
bringing lots of smiles

About the Authors

Lee Gaffney-Lee and her husband, Tom, live in River Ridge, a suburb of New Orleans. They share their home with four rescued mutts-Tallulah Marie, Andrew Thomas, Stanley Watson and Gabrielle Pearl, all of whom work as therapy dogs and hold their Canine Good Citizen titles. A mixed-breed devotee, Lee's personalized license plate reads "MuttNut". Her degree in social work opened her professional life to a variety of careers. Since 1991, Lee has been an active part of the Visiting Pet Program in New Orleans and has served several terms as President. Through the years, she and Tom have rescued, trained and had 12 dogs successfully evaluated for therapy work. Lee is an avid gardener, therapy dog evaluator and trainer.

Lee and Tom with Tallulah, Andy, Stanley and Gabby at "Café Du Mutt", a photography fundraising event to benefit Gulf South Doberman Rescue and the LASPCA.

Malay Ghose-Hajra- Malay is an Assistant Professor in the Civil and Environmental Engineering department at the University of New Orleans in Louisiana. Malay was born and raised in India. He moved to the United States in 1998 for higher education and has lived in this country ever since. Malay joined the Visiting Pet Program in New Orleans in 2007 with his beloved rescued Golden Retriever, Mita. In 2011, Malay added his rescued German Shepherd Dog, Tej, into the VPP program. Malay serves on the board for VPP and regularly participates in their handler orientation, pet-handler evaluation and new volunteer mentoring activities. In his spare time, Malay enjoys travelling, photography, camping, hiking, and motorcycle riding. He lives in Metairie, Louisiana with Mita and Tej.

Malay with Golden Retriever, Mita, and German Shepherd Dog, Tej

Credits

Photography by Stacey Warnke
(www.staceywarnkephotography.com)

A teacher by trade, Stacey not only has a passion for educating today's youth but she also adores animals. She lives in Metairie, LA with three rescued canines and one rescued feline. Her dog, Angelle, is a certified therapy dog with the Visiting Pet Program in New Orleans. As a part-time photographer, Stacey volunteers her skills to the Louisiana SPCA. Capturing tender moments with the ones you love is what Stacey strives to immortalize through her camera.

Angelle and Stacey Warnke
Photo by Terri Joia

Cover Dog –Lilou

Lilou and her mom, Diana María Alcázar-O'Dowd, live in New Orleans. Lilou is part Blue Heeler (Australian cattle dog) and part Beagle. Abandoned in Slidell, LA, she was rescued by the Pontchartrain Humane Society in 2011 and soon adopted by Diana. Lilou was heartworm positive, as well as a very sad and tired girl when rescued. Lots of love, good food and appropriate care allowed her to become the wonderful, enthusiastic and sweet girl she is today. Lilou is a therapy dog with the Visiting Pet Program, participating in visits with both adults and children at hospitals as well as rehabilitation facilities. In her leisure hours, Lilou enjoys stuffed toys, stalking squirrels and participating in the sport of barn hunt. Diana María, born in Bogotá, Colombia, is a D.V.M. and holds a Certificate in Spanish / English Translation and Interpretation from Loyola University of New Orleans. She also currently volunteers at the Stuart H. Smith Law Clinic and Center for Social Justice.

Lilou and Diana O'Dowd

Notes

Notes

Notes

Notes

28627193R00109

Made in the USA
San Bernardino, CA
02 January 2016